WIMBLEDON
2010

THE CHAMPIONSHIPS
WIMBLEDON
OFFICIAL ANNUAL
2010

NEIL HARMAN

Publisher
PPL Sport & Leisure

Managing Director
Bill Cotton

Art Editor
David Kelly

Design Team
Emma Robinson
Graham Nuttall
Caroline O'Donovan

Photography
PA Photos

Editorial
Neil Harman

Copyright (c) 2010
The All England Lawn Tennis
and Croquet Club

Photographs Copyright (c)
PA Photos

This edition
published 2010 by
PPL Sport & Leisure
16 Dempster Building
Atlantic Way
Brunswick Business Park
Liverpool L3 4BE

PPL Sport & Leisure
Bradford House
East Street
Epsom, Surrey KT17 1BL

ISBN 978-1-903381-21-2

Printed by Scotprint
East Lothian EH41 3ST

ROLEX

CONTENTS

FOREWORD

Tim Phillips

Chairman of The All England Lawn Tennis and Croquet Club
and Committee of Management of The Championships

The 124th Championships were memorable in many ways. Our new retractable roof, designed to provide rain cover, became instead a moveable sunshade because it did not rain at all. We saw the fastest ever Centre Court serve and the latest ever play (Novak Djokovic finally defeated Olivier Rochus at 10:58 pm in his first round match).

On Court 18 we saw the longest tennis match ever played, between John Isner and Nicolas Mahut which lasted 11 hours and 5 minutes with the former finally winning 70-68 in the fifth set. This truly unbelievable match, which was played with great skill, sportsmanship and competitive intensity, was 71 games longer than the longest ever previous match at Wimbledon going back to 1877 – and remember tie breaks in the first four sets were only introduced at Wimbledon in 1971.

The icing on the cake for Wimbledon in 2010 was the visit of The Queen, Patron of the All England Club. She walked through the grounds before play began on the first Thursday and received a very warm welcome from fans and top ranked international players alike. This visit made for an extremely happy day and after lunch it was made happier still for British

fans by Andy Murray who beat Jarkko Nieminen with The Queen watching. She met both players afterwards on the Royal Box balcony.

We were delighted to welcome as official guests this year two former American greats who were celebrating the 60th anniversary of Championship singles wins here in 1950 – Louise Brough and Budge Patty. They were joined by two former Australian champions – Neale Fraser celebrating the 50th anniversary of his win and Evonne Goolagong Cawley, the last mother to win the Wimbledon Ladies' singles title who was celebrating the 30th anniversary of her second win at Wimbledon.

Throughout Wimbledon 2010 the quality of the tennis matched the sunny weather. There were epic matches from first to last, when Rafael Nadal and Serena Williams, the two top ranked players in the world finally emerged as richly deserving champions – in both senses because they each won £1 million.

All this, and much more, is captured in the words and photos which follow. I hope this annual will bring back many happy memories for you of Wimbledon 2010.

INTRODUCTION Neil Harman, The Times

That there was no Englishman in the main draw for the men's singles at this year's Championships – the first time that had happened in its 133 year history – was greeted with a sense of sadness that would not easily be assuaged. There were plenty of chaps who would come through the gates in the next fortnight who could play the game and the All England Club's Road to Wimbledon junior initiative was the finest of its kind in the country but, as in all good things, time was of the essence. The fruits of the Club's labours would be borne sometime in the future – of that there was no doubt.

The lack of a local dialect at one's home tournament was hurtful to those of us in-bred in the sport but we had Andy Murray and Jamie Baker, from Scotland, to do us proud, one by virtue of being the No.4 player in the world and now twice a Grand Slam finalist and the other thanks to a wild card invitation from the club. Baker had overcome a life-threatening blood illness which had deprived him of at least a year of his careeer and so, at 23, it was like he was starting out again. Murray had once said that if all the professionals in the world were like Jamie Baker, tennis would be a better place and so echoed all of us.

There was a greater degree of positive feelings on the women's side, six British players were in the starting line-up, both Elena Baltacha and Anne Keothavong by virtue of their ranking – though only Baltacha was inside the world's top 100 and threatening to break into the best 50 – and four others, Katie O'Brien, Laura Robson, Mel South and Heather Watson thanks to invitations.

Most attention, of course, landed upon Murray who had experienced a difficult clay court season after beginning the year in such rich form that he had reached the final of the mixed Hopman Cup event in Perth and flown east from there to perform beautifully in the Australian Open, where his levels were such that a British victory was not out of the question until he just started to question himself against Roger Federer in the final. One did not do that and live to tell a tale of success.

Murray was not able to successfully defend his AEGON title at Queen's Club, either, beaten by Mardy Fish, of the United States, in a match that was stopped for darkness on Wednesday night and was completed in a flash of errors from the Scot's racket in the decisive tie-break early on Thursday afternoon. Yet, a few days later, he was seated around a table for a social evening with the ever decreasing number of British tennis correspondents, a moment when we could relax in each other's company and tell it how it really was. Murray was in an excellent mood. It augured well.

And, of course, there was another sporting event taking place at the same time. "I've been in that same goldfish bowl before Wimbledon, so I know what it's like, and I think it will be marginally easier for Murray with the expectations that bit lower," said Tim Henman, a member of the Wimbledon management committee, who played in four semi-finals at the All England Lawn Tennis Club.

"When it's a World Cup year, it's maybe a little more relaxed. But, as a player, you have to try to be oblivious to everything that is going on around you. The more you can be unaware of everything that is happening, the better it is."

Hard to think that Murray would be unaware of what was expected of him, for he expected precisely the same of himself. He knew that he had been criticised for being too negative in certain passages of play; people felt he ought to take the game to the opposition but that was often easier said than done. He just wanted to get out and play.

And Grand Slam finals would not be a surprise to him any more. "I like being nervous going into matches. It shows that you care and that you're ready. And if you feel like you're going to win, you're going to be nervous. Before the (2008) US Open I felt like I could win, but the final (against Roger Federer) came round really, really quickly after the high of the Nadal match. I don't know if I was necessarily physically fatigued, but to beat those two guys back-to-back you need to be pretty much perfect. I don't think I was ready then to win a Grand Slam.

"At the Australian Open this year, I felt like I was ready, physically, and my game was there to win. I was definitely more nervous for that final, but in a good way. I wasn't feeling like the occasion was going to get the better of me or anything like that."

Federer, having reached the final of the US Open – where he was beaten by Juan Martin del Potro, who had been sadly absent from the sport for six months with a right wrist injury – earned his 16th Grand Slam in Melbourne but had been beaten in the quarter-finals of the French Open by Robin Soderling, the hugely powerful Swede.

As he strolled through the grounds a few days before The Championships, greeting members, flower waterers and weed extractors alike, could anyone seem less like tennis's greatest accumulator of titles? Federer was classically cool, uninhibited by the demands upon him. On the day before the curtain went up he fulfilled his usual round of press obligations, dressed in his gold-flecked RF tracksuit topped off with a light-grey scarf.

The invigoration of a return to Wimbledon, the memories it invokes, of the incredible highs – six titles, a victory over Pete Sampras in 2001 when he was a kid with a dodgy complexion, a pony-tail and an eye for greatness – and the occasional low like having to watch Rafael Nadal clamber across the Centre Court parapets two years before, lifts him. "So beautiful," he says, "I love how the place looks, everything just blends in, how they do the new courts, the flowers, the people always are so chilled."

Indeed they are. The grounds looked particularly glorious this year, the foundations for the new Court No.3 were in place and if the Club would allow me a particular grievance (I loved the old Court 2 with its standing area at the top, its wonderful character, the memories it evoked) I was sure the new structure would grow on me in time.

There was no doubting the character of the men's and women's fields. Federer was here, Rafael Nadal had returned after missing the opportunity to defend his title in 2009, Andy Roddick would attempt to win the title for the 10th time (which deserved a medal for gallantry if nothing else), there were 14 Spaniards, assorted new players from Lithuania and Kazakhstan, Uzbekistan and Jamaica (but no English!!). But the men's draw had lost some real draw cards. Ernests Gulbis, the brilliant Latvian, succumbed to a hamstring injury, Richard Gasquet, the 2007 semi-finalist to knee problems.

Quite remarkably, the Williams sisters were the No.1 and No.2 seeds in the women's singles, something that had not happened since 2002, when Venus was one and Serena two. They had swopped places this year for the sake of variety. The Belgians were back, too. Kim Clijsters and Justine Henin embellished the draw, having not been at the event for four and three years respectively. Clijsters had been drawn back to tennis by the invitation of the All England Club to participate in the mixed doubles event which raised the Centre Court roof in May last year.

"Wimbledon's always been the Slam where I would've looked to do better," the US Open champion said. "When you've won before you want to relive those emotions and to do so at Wimbledon would be incredible. I was there with my dad every year. (Leo, her father, died of cancer at the start of 2009) That was a very intense relationship and during those two weeks we were both so proud to be there, so excited.

"It will be emotionally a little harder not to have him there but it's something I look forward to playing again. The tradition is incredible, so Wimbledon is definitely the one I really enjoy."

And so said all of us. There was no richer event to attend in terms of what it offered the general public, no event for which there was a greater sense of the mix of tradition and contemporary virtues, where history and happiness sat together so comfortably. And, of course, we had the added bonus this year of the best of all royal patronages with Her Majesty The Queen having a trip to the grounds in her diary for Thursday the 24th.

Virginia Wade, whom The Queen had witnessed winning the title on her last visit 33 years ago, was all of a flutter. "That year I had my lucky dress with the pink details that I kept washing and wearing for every match and when I looked up to the Royal Box, the Queen was wearing exactly the same pink so I thought 'that's a good sign.'" That was not something that Murray, having been drawn in the bottom half of the draw and therefore a strong possibility for Thursday's card, could get himself too worked up about.

He just wanted to win. No bias intended but we wanted it for him, too.

THE WIMBLEDON CHAMPIONSHIPS

THE ALL ENGLAND LAWN TENNIS
AND CROQUET CLUB
LONDON, ENGLAND
JUNE 21ST TO JULY 4TH, 2010

Inscribed above the players' entrance to Centre Court is the biggest "If" in all of sport. Few will ever earn the right to see Kipling's words there. But those who do will know they're not about winning or losing. They're about the greatness that comes from honouring the game. When walking on to the grass of Centre Court, one senses honour is the name of the game. That and an unbreakable will to win.

ROLEX. A CROWN FOR EVERY ACHIEVEMENT.

OYSTER PERPETUAL DATEJUST II

"IF YOU CAN MEET WITH TRIUMPH AND DISASTER
AND TREAT THOSE TWO IMPOSTORS JUST THE SAME"

ROLEX

Roger Federer

Seeded 1st.

Age: 28. Born: Basel, Switzerland

Since the 2009 Championships and 11 years after he had won the boys' singles title here, Federer had become the father of twin girls, lost in the final of the US Open to Juan Martin Del Potro, taken on, and beaten, all comers in the Australian Open, including Andy Murray in the final, which meant he was the proud bearer of 16 Grand Slam singles titles but, two weeks before the event, had forfeited his world No.1 ranking to Rafael Nadal. He said he had been suffering from a lung infection earlier in the year that probably accounted for a poor sequence of results coming into Wimbledon, including his loss in the final of the Halle grass court event to Lleyton Hewitt.

Rafael Nadal

Seeded 2nd.

Age 24: Born Manacor, Majorca, Spain.

Having missed last year's Championships, this remarkable athlete from the Balearics had been troubled through the second half of 2009 and not until he reach the final of the Shanghai Masters did he feel good about himself again. He sparked further fears about his knees by retiring in the quarter-finals of the Australian Open against Andy Murray when two sets down but he had given himself a look in during the early spring stretch and then dazzled on clay, dropping two sets in winning the five tournaments he played, including a fifth Roland Garros in quite breathtaking fashion. He was world No.1 but had been demoted to No.2 seed by the implementation of the Club's grass-court formula.

Novak Djokovic
Seeded 3rd.

Age: 23. Born: Belgrade, Serbia.

What to make of Novak Djokovic? Forever there or thereabouts at the top of the game but unable to command the kind of attention that was the norm for Federer and Nadal, it was unremittingly tough to be Djokovic. He had played in only one final in 2010, in Dubai on hard courts in February and had since stumbled to some difficult defeats, even having to retire during the tournament in Belgrade, on clay, that was run by his family. At Queen's, two weeks before The Championships, he was defeated by Xavier Malisse, of Belgium, in the third round and though one tried to console him in the players' room afterwards, he seemed very down. He remained passionately committed to winning Wimbledon.

Andy Murray
Seeded 4th.

Age: 23. Born: Dunblane, Scotland

Two weeks after last year's Championships, Murray had turned out for the North of Scotland in the LTA County Cup at Eastbourne, so he was becoming quite a character. He had risen to No.2 in the world rankings in August 2009, was a main attraction at the Barclays ATP World Tour finals at the O2 in November and, come January, having played in his first Hyundai Hopman Cup in partnership with Laura Robson (they reached the final) he became a finalist at the Australian Open for the first time, losing to Federer. A quiet period since, a fourth round defeat to Tomas Berdych, of the Czech Republic, at the French Open, and optimism was not quite as high for Murray's prospects as it had been a year earlier.

Andy Roddick

Seeded 5th.

Age: 27. Born: Omaha, Nebraska, USA

Almost every other week of his life someone would remind the American that he had been a part of a remarkable 2009 men's final, he would smile for a while and then the hurt would kick in. He did not want to become synonymous with one defeat. Having won his first tournament of the year, in Brisbane, he then had an exemplary spring in his home country, reaching the final in Indian Wells and defeating Berdych in the final in Miami, which suggested he was feeling sharp. He then decided to miss almost the entire clay court season, to go on holiday, re-appearing at Roland Garros, where he lost in the third round to Russian, Teimuraz Gabashvili. A second round loss at Queen's to Israel's Dudi Sela, certainly raised eyebrows.

Robin Soderling

Seeded 6th.

Age: 25. Born: Tibro, Sweden

Now established inside the top ten, he had made his first significant impression when he ended Rafael Nadal's run of 31 straight victories at Roland Garros in 2009 and where he ultimately reached the final. This boy hits the ball like a rocket, especially on the forehand, and the grass courts held no fears for him, though he had not been further than the fourth round in seven visits. At the French Open this year, he defeated Roger Federer in the quarter-finals but fell to Nadal in the final, though it needed the very best from the Spaniard to hold him at bay. The Swedes were getting pretty excited that Soderling could end their 20 year wait for a men's singles champion.

Nikolay Davydenko

Seeded 7th.

Age: 29. Born: Severodonezk, Ukraine

Davydenko liked the London air as had been demonstrated when he lifted the inaugural Barclays ATP World tour finals at the 02 last November. Then he won Doha in the first week of the year in spectacular fashion and we thought this might be a stellar year only for him to be struck down by a wrist injury that was initially diagnosed as not a major concern but, after an MRI, was diagnosed as a fracture. As such, Davydenko did not play from March until his return to the grass court championships in Halle where he was beaten in the second round by Benjamin Becker of Germany. It was hard to see him making much of an impact at The Championships.

Fernando Verdasco

Seeded 8th.

Age: 26. Born: Madrid, Spain.

Verdasco had been a there or thereabouts figure for a long time now, without being able to make that decisive, major breakthrough. He played a lot of clay court tennis in the spring, winning Barcelona, and reaching the final in Nice and the semi-finals in Rome but it was the Monte Carlo final, when he won just a single game from Rafael Nadal that lived longer in the memory. He had chosen not to play any grass court tennis at all in the build up to The Championships which made you wonder how highly he rated his chances of lasting more than a week.

Serena Williams

Seeded 1st.

Age: 28. Born: Saginaw, Michigan, USA

Remarkably, the three-time former champion had played just five tournaments in 2010 prior to entering The Championships. Through a mixture of knee injuries and a desire to play a nominal calendar, Serena stopped off in Rome, Madrid and Paris after her victorious march through the Australian Open in January, where she defeated Justine Henin in a memorable final. Since last year's triumph over her sister, Venus, in the final, Serena had been involved in a sensational US Open when, in the semi-final against Kim Clijsters, she was foot faulted on the penultimate point which provoked an outburst against the lineswoman, a hefty fine and a warning as to her future conduct.

Venus Williams

Seeded 2nd.

Age: 30. Born: Lynwood, California, USA.

Having won this title five times in the past 10 years, it was a tremendous tribute to Venus that she was among the favoured again, this time as the No.2 seed, the first time since 2002 that Venus and Serena had been the top two seeds. After reaching the quarter-finals at the Australan Open in January (where she lost to China's Li Na), Venus won on hard courts in Dubai, and on clay in Acapulco, as well as the finals in Miami and Madrid. It had been a varied build up but, as usual, you could discount previous results when it came to Venus on grass.

Caroline Wozniacki

Seeded 3rd.

Age: 19. Born:Odense, Denmark

As opposed to Serena Williams playing five tournaments in the six months leading into Wimbledon, Wozniacki had been involved in 13. There was more than one way to skin a cat. The teenager, who reached the final of the US Open in September, where she lost to Kim Clijsters, was a real trouper of the tour and one hoped she did not over-play. She had played only one grass court match in the Wimbledon build up, losing to Aravane Rezai, of France, in the first round in Eastbourne. The Danes had never had a Grand Slam champion and poured a lot of hopes upon Wozniacki's young shoulders.

Jelena Jankovic

Seeded 4th.

Age: 25. Born: Belgrade, Serbia

A sum total of two finals – she won on the hard courts in Indian Wells, California – and one semi-final had been the lot of this gifted, but so often over-wrought, player from Serbia in 2010. The latest in a long line of disappointments in the Grand Slams had come at Roland Garros two weeks before The Championships, where Jankovic dropped one set in reaching the semi-finals and won only three games against Australia's Samantha Stosur there. It was hard to believe that she had begun 2009 as the No.1 player in the world because there did seem something fundamentally flawed in her character.

Francesca Schiavone
Seeded 5th.

Age: 29. Born: Milan, Italy

How vivacious, how exhilarating had been Schiavone's victory in the French Open, the first by an Italian woman in a Grand Slam championship and one of such self-possession and joy. Schiavone would be 30 on the first Wednesday of The Championships but age had only served to enhance her prospects, not diminish them. This would be her tenth Championships and this player with a glorious single-handed backhand had reached a career best quarter-final in 209. Notthing had prepared her for the tumult that followed her success in Paris and in her single outing on grass, at Eastbourne, she was beaten by Romania's Sorana Cirstea.

Samantha Stosur
Seeded 6th.

Age: 26 Born: Brisbane, Australia

A Roland Garros semi-final in 209 was followed by her appearance in the French final a year on where she had played with such distinction to get to the last day, only to fall to Schiavone's bewitching performance. Stosur had wondered about how well her game would transfer from clay to grass for, unlike so many Australians, she found movement across the lawns to be more difficult, though she had reached the quarter-finals in Eastbourne. It had been a particularly stand out year, though, for a player who prided herself upon her physical strength and agility.

Agnieszka Radwanska

Seeded 7th.

Age: 21 Born: Krakow, Poland

One of the new guard of the women's game, if a rather unexciting performer, Radwanska had reached the quarter-finals on her previous two appearances in SW19 and was being pencilled in as a possible challenger for a spot in the last four. This was her highest seeding in a Grand Slam tournament even though she had not been able to reach a final at all on the tour during 2010. She had a feisty competitive spirit but one wondered whether she truly believed in her status as a top ten player. Like so many players on tour, she preferred the baseline to coming forward.

Kim Clijsters

Seeded 8th.

Age: 27 Born: Bilzen, Belgium

And so here was the bubbly Clijsters, having returned to the sport thanks to the invitation to play in the Wimbledon Centre Court roof raising of May last year, having won the US Open in glorious style in September and having moved steathily up the rankings to where she was being noted as a potential champion in SW19, something she proudly said she had set her heart on. There was not a better ball striker in the game but having missed four Wimbledons in succession, you wondered if it might take her a bit longer to adjust to this surface than any other.

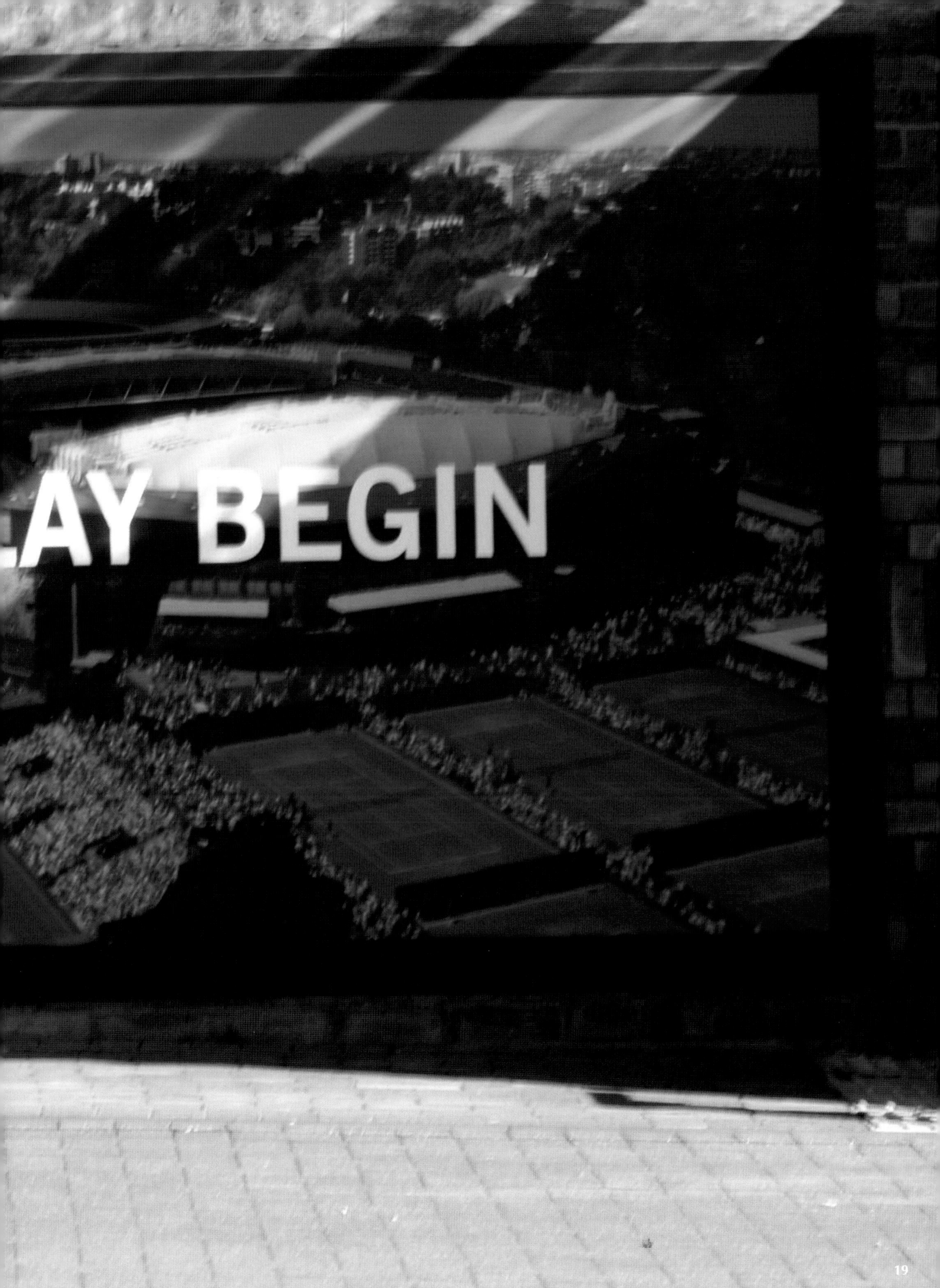
AY BEGIN

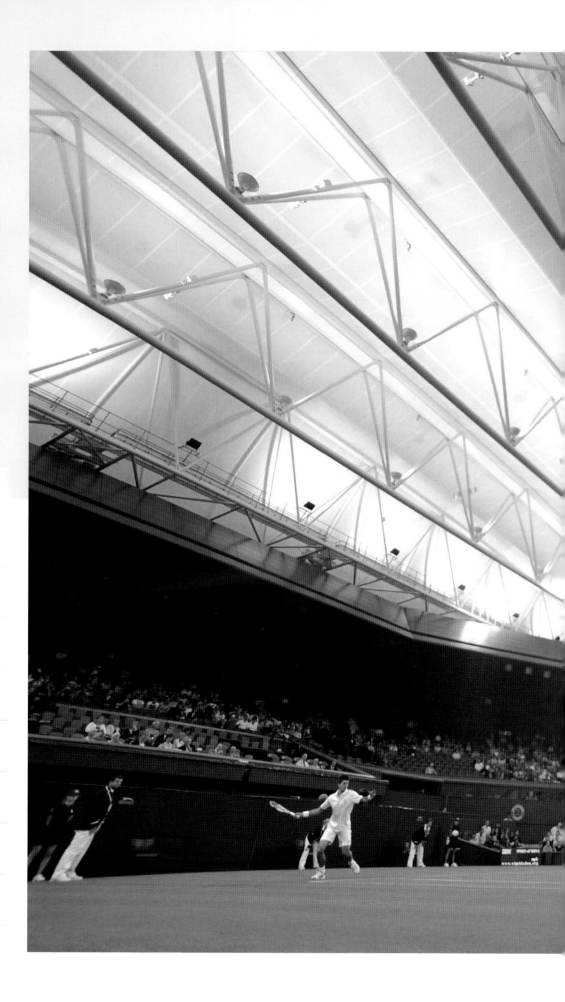

It opened on the Summer Solstice beneath a burnishing sun and closed at two minutes to 11pm, the roof drawn across Centre Court, the air controlled and not a raindrop in the forecast for the rest of the week. Days at The Championships did not come much more redolent, breathtaking, valiant and controversial at that which heralded the opening of the 124th version.

Novak Djokovic, the Serbian No.3 seed, was the last man to settle on his place in the second round, defeating Olivier Rochus, a Belgian short on inches but high on skills, 4-6 6-2 3-6 6-4 6-2. "It was interesting", Djokovic said. "You don't get to see a lot of late night matches in Wimbledon history – I'm happy in a way that my name is in the history books of playing late in the night."

Andrew Jarrett, the referee, had chosen to inform both players at 8.30 pm that the light was fading and he preferred to finish the match under the roof. It would take 30 minutes for the effects to kick in but he determined there was no other course open to him. Rochus was leading by two sets to one and had the momentum; Djokovic did not mind stopping and rejuvenating in the least. When the pair returned, Djokovic started the brighter and managed to complete his victory at two minutes to 11, when a curfew imposed at the behest of Merton Borough Council would have required play to be suspended for the sake of the local residents. Jarrett, and a fair few others, breathed an audible sigh of relief for that would have been a slice of notoriety Wimbledon did not want.

Novak Djokovic

Olivier Rochus

The place reeked of history of course, it flowed through every nook and cranny. It is what made the place the wonder that it has remained all these years. Roger Federer knew all about that. As he walked the corridor of champions to Centre Court to begin Monday's proceedings once again, he sensed he was ready for the occasion. "There are always nerves involved. It means the world to me to open up on Centre. It's a dream for any player. When I walked out, I was thinking 'this court is amazing'. I don't remember it ever being so perfect."

Federer sought perfection in all things. But three hours and 18 minutes after Sweden's Lars Graff, who umpired last year's men's singles final, had flicked his coin into the air, the Swiss was counting his blessings that he did not have to consider moving out of his temporary home in the village having only just made himself and his family comfortable.

Alejandro Falla, of Colombia, ranked No.65 in the world, served for the story of this and any other Wimbledon Championship at 5-4 in the fourth set. He had won the first two sets and, at 4-4 in the third, had love-40 on the Federer serve. We were sharpening our nibs, our knives, too. Falla is

pronounced 'fi-yah.' You could imagine the headlines that were being prepared in newspaper offices across the world.

So here we were at the point of no return (or in Federer's case, the point of as many returns as he could get his racket on). The Colombian did not start well, a backhand error then one on the forehand, and you wondered if he had suddenly begun to play the man rather than the ball.

Then Federer netted a backhand, but responded with an outrageous backhand drop shot to which – though Falla managed to keep the point alive – Federer flicked a winner into the open court. An ace preserved one break point, but the Swiss was able to generate a bit more pace off the ground in the ensuing rally and Falla's footwork was sloppy, he lost his direction on a forehand and Federer's roar almost blew Princess Michael of Kent's hat away.

Even then, in the next game, Falla squeezed what was to be his last opportunity. He had a break point, it was on his racket, a backhand down the line was his to make. Time seemed to stand still for a second. He missed it. The tie-break disappeared all too quickly, the final set lasted only 27 minutes and that was because there were ➤

Roger Federer

six deuces in the sixth game. Survival had been secured. The tournament breathed again.

Only twice in 133 Wimbledons had the defending champion suffered a first round exit (Manuel Santana in 1967 to Charlie Pasarell and Lleyton Hewitt to Ivo Karlovic in 2003) but they were both one-term winners, not the serial collector of titles of Federer's class. "For me it's not normal to be down two sets to love, especially at Wimbledon but however I felt out there, I managed to find a way to win and that's the most important thing."

For Falla, being the first day's almost golden boy seemed to be enough recompense. "I am happy that today I played a great match," he said. "Today is a special day for me in tennis, even if I lost. I can say I was serving for the match against Federer and many players would like to be in that situation."

Andy Roddick, the man who had lost the tumultuous final against Federer a year ago, did

Alejandro Falla

Andy Roddick

not have quite such a start on the opening day of his 10th Wimbledon challenge. In fact, it was the nearest anyone came to routine on the opening day, a 6-3 6-2 6-2 victory over his fellow American, Rajeev Ram. And this was not just Roddick at his punishing, intimidating best. As Julian Muscat in *The Times* wrote, "The way he picked Ram's pocket at the start of the second set would have animated the Artful Dodger. Roddick joked once that he was the 'best bad player in the world' but truth is the bedrock of sharp humour."

Boy, how those followers of the British game needed a sense of humour on Day One. Elena Baltacha, the British No.1 and Laura Robson, the girl who everyone assumes will be Britain's No.1 one day, both bade farewell to the singles competition. Baltacha lost 2-6, 7-5, 6-3 to Petra Martic, a 19-year-old from Croatia, having served for the match at 5-4 in the second set. "I tried to stay as relaxed as I could but I did get quite tight," she said. "I'm human. I'm not a machine."

It was, as Patrick Kidd in *The Times* pointed out, from "Bally Hoo to Bally High and finally Bally Hell". Having reached the quarter finals in Eastbourne the previous week, the positive vibes from Baltacha were all powerful but, as so often happened at the major to end all majors, something gave out. For almost two sets she played like someone who believed that a run at The Championships was no fantasy – until she served for the match against the waif-like Martic and then, like Alice in Wonderland, she woke up.

Robson was afforded centre stage and what a match to savour, against Jelena Jankovic the world No.4 from Serbia who, if things did not go her way, might drop her service, droop her shoulders

Rajeev Ram

and generally dissolve into a hissy fit. At first, anyway, Jankovic made a bit of a thing of pulling rank, swanning out in a sort of 'I'm a top player' tutu, doing her level best in the warm up and knocking off the first two games in four minutes. But then Robson began to warm up. And then she started swinging.

In the juniors, she was akin to a flat track bully. Alas, it was not easy to bully players in the top ten, unless your name is Williams. So Robson had the comparatively novel experience of getting as good as she gave and better. Jankovic also liked to hit a deep ball and did so without restraint. And so a 6-3 7-6 defeat was a tough lesson for Robson but one that she would undoubtedly take on board and would make her stronger in the future.

"The court wasn't as overwhelming as I thought it would be," she said, which was an encouragingly upbeat thought. "It's not as big as it looks on TV. And I think I could have played a bit better. I think I can improve on everything, really."

Robson, Baltacha, Mel South and Katie O'Brien (though the latter put up a sterling effort before losing to Alona Bondarenko the No.28 seed from Ukraine in near darkness on No.15 Court) were in good company as they departed the scene. A mere 23 days had passed since Francesca Schiavone, of Italy, had become an unheralded champion on clay at Roland Garros. We loved the way she played, the way she spoke, the gaiety of her personality. Was this the same Schiavone who appeared on No.2 court, making 38 unforced errors, losing it with herself, her coach, the umpire and the ball girls?

Left: Laura Robson

Below: Sir Clive Woodward

Her fury was initially sparked by a faulty PA system which insisted on broadcasting the score from Nikolay Davydenko's match against Kevin Anderson at random intervals (Davydenko won from two sets down, 9-7 in the fifth). Schiavone really let the situation affect her concentration, sometimes the rage worked for her but, for the most part, it aided her opponent, the Russian Vera Dushevina, the 2002 junior champion. "It was a tough match on a different court with a different feeling", said Schiavone, who lost 6-7 7-5 6-1 to the world No.47.

Strolling the outside courts on the opening day was one of those 'must-do' experiences, the sardine-like closeness of the courts and the

Dustin Brown

people, being stopped every once in a while by a lost soul who thought your press pass was a steward's insignia, and stumbling upon a player you had not seen before.

One such was Dustin Brown, a Jamaican who had a German mother and paternal British grandparents, playing in the main draw for the first time. The British scouts were sniffing because Brown had become frustrated at the lack of support from his home federation who sent him a message two days before the event congratulating him on his wild card into Wimbledon, whereas he had earned a place in the main draw by right.

Ivan Speck, in the *Daily Mail*, also found Brown eminently watchable. "His quirks include asking for the same ball back after winning a point. In one particular service game, which he held to love, he used the same ball on four points. He wears a fluorescent green shoelace on his right shoe and a fluorescent orange shoelace on his left, laces he borrowed one when he turned up to a tournament without any." What a shame that he should lost 6-3 4-6 6-2 6-3 to Austria's Jurgen Melzer, a recent French Open semi-finalist, for we'd have liked to have seen more of him.

As we would have of Stanislas Wawrinka, who competed in one of the most memorable matches of the 2009 Championships, the under-the-roof experience against Andy Murray in the fourth round. This time, Wawrinka did not get past the first, beaten 6-7 6-1 2-6 7-6 6-3 by Denis Istomin of Uzbekistan, who had caught the eye at Queen's, where he had given Rafael Nadal a real fright. *Au revoir*, Stan.

QUOTE of the Day

KIM CLIJSTERS, OF BELGIUM, WHO DEFEATED MARINA ELENA CAMERIN, OF ITALY, 6-0 6-3 LOST HER SENSE OF DIRECTION ON THE WAY TO NO.2 COURT AND HAD TO ASK A STEWARD FOR DIRECTIONS.

"Just nerves I suppose, I guess you can compare it to your first day of school after a school holiday. It's exciting and curious, you get a lot of emotions. And it's that mixture going on in your head that makes you more nervous than usual."

Day **TWO**
22.06.2010

FOGNINI
VS
VERDASCO

NADAL
VS
NISHIKORI

MURRAY
VS
HAJEK

RODIONOVA
VS
KEOTHAVONG

BAKER
VS
BECK

BLAKE
VS
HAASE

S.WILLIAMS
VS
LARCHER DE BRITO

STOSUR
VS
KANEPI

Tuesday 22 June…

It was as if the prospective grass court supremos in the men's draw who had witnessed Roger Federer's extraordinary fright on the opening day had come together and decided, "This is not going to happen to me". Unfortunately, not everyone had been taking enough care of what could occur when the grass was still bedding down and one's opponent came out with a glint in his eye.

Rafael Nadal, Robin Soderling, protagonists in the recent French Open final, Sam Querrey, the Queen's Club champion, and, to the eternal gratitude of the nation, Andy Murray, all came and claimed victory with a briskness that did them credit and pleased us wordsmiths as well. There were casualties we had not expected; Fernando Verdasco, the No.8 seed, Juan Carlos Ferrero, twice a former quarter-finalist and Guillermo Garcia-Lopez, the Eastbourne runner-up, all disappeared. There was a significant Spanish lament.

Not least in the offices of the *Daily Mail* which had signed Verdasco for an *In The Locker Room* set of features they hoped would last for longer than one edition. His first – and last - report was a classic. "We had the chance to get a house near the All England Club this year but my father didn't really like the idea," Verdasco wrote. "It would be difficult to find somewhere to eat every night, plus we would have to clean and look after the house – and we don't want to be doing that!"

Fortunately for the non-domesticated Verdasco clan, they didn't have to pay much for the phalanx of hotel rooms they had booked either, for the bread-winner was on his way out after one match, defeated by an indefatigable performance from Fabio Fognini, the Italian who had previously won only a single match on the grounds. Red faces all around.

At least Nadal did his stuff, and how well he did it against Kei Nishikori, the Japanese wild card, prompting Julian Muscat in *The Times* to suggest that it was just as well for Spanish bulls that the 2008 champion had never embraced the *corrida*. "He chose instead to play tennis and condemns opponents to death by a thousand metaphorical cuts."

Nishikori was in the main draw as a nod towards the importance of Asia in terms of the promotion of Wimbledon as a major sporting event, and because he had been unable to compete in three of the four Grand Slam tournaments in 2009 with an elbow injury from which he had recovered by March. Nishikori was determined to make the most of his first Centre Court opportunity, knowing in his hearts of hearts that it would probably be a relatively short one.

He was a boisterous, lively, jack-a-napes opponent for Nadal, a tricky assignment for the world No.1 who knew he would have to concentrate on what he was doing from first to last. First things first and having broken the Nishikori serve in the opening game, an immediate sense of destiny fell across Centre Court. Nadal won 6-2 6-4 6-4. ➤

Fabio Fognini

Kei Nishikori

Rafael Nadal

We hoped that the same would be true over on No.1 Court where Murray was beginning his quest against Jan Hajek, the world No.67 from the Czech Republic who gave the impression of being a decent opponent against whom to measure your readiness for such an event. He was good, but not too good.

Whoops; Murray was broken in the third game of the match with a delicate dink drop shot by Hajek that belied his swarthy, lusty groundstroke-type appearance. Fortunately, Murray then eased our heightening nerves by breaking in the eighth game to level and then pinning Hajek to the back of the court with relentless length off the ground. Suddenly, the British No.1 was off on a stretch of seven successive games and the tide of the match was inexorably turned for him to enjoy a relatively painless 7-5 6-1 6-2 victory.

Kevin Mitchell, in *The Guardian*, recognised the importance of the victory and its manner. "The crowd on No.1 court – not quite as corporate or celebrity-laden as Centre – rose to greet a convincing return of form by a player who has stuttered into the affections of the nation. It remains a mystery why pockets of Planet Tennis set their hard face against him. Jokes about ABM (Anyone But Murray) T-shirts outlive their mirth pretty quickly, although he seems unconcerned."

When Murray came off court, though, he was a single ray of sunshine on another dark day for the home nation in their own championships, the return of one victory from eight in the singles representing the worst record in the event's history. All around in the press room, the sages of the domestic game who were considered as *persona non grata* by the governing body gathered to pay what seemed like their last respects for British tennis, and wonder when someone would take the bull by the horns and do something credible for its future.

Simon Barnes, in *The Times*, referred to PBs – Plucky Brits - as he wrote "Over here in the London Borough of Merton, there have been an awful lot of people suffering under the unbearable heaviness of being expected to play reasonably well at a professional sporting event. Anne Keothavong, Plucky Brit, blew a 4-0 lead in the final set and said: 'There's so much pressure on us all here.'" ➤

Anne Keothavong

Jan Hajek

Jamie Baker

Andy Murray

"Now hear a plain fact; all athletes must bear the weight of expectation. It's part of the job, like accountants being able to do sums and journalists being able to write quickly. Being able to bear the weight of expectation is a basic requirement of success. The better you are, the greater the weight you must bear and the better you must be at bearing it. Do you think Rafael Nadal bears no weight of expectation? Or Roger Federer? Or Brazil? Or Argentina?"

The LTA's player director, Steve Martens, suggested that the results, a series of calamitous reverses, were 'not a reflection on British tennis.' So what were they a reflection of, one wondered.

We did not like the result but equally, the behaviour of some of those who took it out on our players was not exactly likeable either. Anastasia Rodionova, the world No.74 from Australia, for instance, who won the last six games of the match to defeat Keothavong, behaved throughout like a spoiled brat, moaning at every line call not given in her favour, gesticulating, arguing, and generally doing all she could to unsettle her opponent. One made a mental note of hoping she might get her comeuppance relatively quickly.

Onto the same court, came Jamie Baker, hoping to turn around the local fortunes. Baker, the Glaswegian ranked No.254 the week of The Championships and thus just outside the criteria of No.250 which was the LTA's modest cut-off for players to be recommended for a wild card, but the Club chose to give him one in any case. Baker succumbed in straight sets, to Andreas Beck, the left hander from Germany.

The sorriest story of the second day was the defeat of James Blake, a player who really ought to have made more of his game on the biggest stages of the world than three quarter-finals, one in New York and the other in Melbourne. For some reason – hard to fathom really because he possessed a game that should have transferred well to grass (he was a former AEGON championship finalist at Queen's remember) simply failed to sparkle in SW19. He had only played in the third round twice in seven previous visits.

This time, he was defeated in straight sets, 6-2 6-4 6-4 by Robin Haase, of the Netherlands, in the midst of which he looked up to where Pam Shriver, the former doubles champion, and now a commentator for his home American audience, was speaking in what he clearly thought were distracting tones. "You played tennis and I can still hear you," Blake yelled. More polite later, he seemed resigned also, that tendinitis in his knee would plague what was left of his career at the age of 30.

"It isn't great," he said. "If it doesn't get better soon I'm not sure how much longer I want to play in pain. I can't beat these guys at 80 per cent. I can't even beat a lot of them at 100 per cent on a given day."

Serena Williams

Blake's contemporary, Robby Ginepri, who had reached a career-best fourth round at the French Open before losing to Novak Djokovic, also stumbled at the first hurdle, though it was hardly unexpected for his opponent was Soderling, the Swedish No.6 seed, who lost only seven games in an hour and 18 minutes.

On what was Ladies Day, with the defending champion taking the obligatory centre stage, Serena Williams did not disappoint. She faced Michelle Larcher De Brito, a young Portuguese who had been renowned in the past for the deafening noise she made as she prepared to make contact with, made contact with and after she made contact with, the ball. Fortunately, for the crowd, she did not make contact with much this day.

Serena rolled the teenager 6-0, 6-4 and said her only disappointment was that she ought to have come to the net more. That is what it is with these champions – they can never be satisfied.

Samantha Stosur had warned us during her fine run at Roland Garros, where she reached the final, that she was not your typical Aussie female who came over all unnecessary when it was time to play on grass. We did not expect her to stumble so soon, though, the No.6 seed losing in straight sets to Kaia Kanepi, an Estonian qualifier. She said she did not think she had to drastically change anything in her game to be ultra competitive on grass – 'I just have to get better at it," Stosur said.

Maria Sharapova, the Russian, dropped one game to her compatriot, Anastasia Pivovarova and Caroline Wozniacki, the Danish No.3 seed, forfeited two to Tathiana Garbin of Italy. Oh and a match started on Court No.18 at around 6pm between John Isner, the American, and Nicolas Mahut, of France, for which one of those would receive the same recompense as a first round loser in the men's singles as Miss Pivovarova and Miss Garbin received for their minor contributions in the women's event. We were to hear more of Isner and Mahut as the days dragged by.

QUOTE of the Day

"We dubbed it Strawberries and Cream. Straw - berries is the proper enunciation of it. I don't have a good British accent. The red is strawberries and the white is cream. It's not like a pure white. The red symbolises a lot of things I do in Africa – everybody that buys a pair can pretty much save a life in Africa. I really wanted to tie all this together. I should have had a strawberry design on my nails too, but I went for hearts."

Samantha Stosur

Kaia Kanepi

Michelle Larcher De Brito

Maria Sharapova

John Isner

"Game Without End" was the *Daily Mail's* banner headline. **"Yawn Tennis,"** uttered the *Daily Telegraph*, which suggested that particular newspaper was spent of both energy and inspiration on a third day of The Championships that was to be without parallel in the long and virtuous history of the sport.

For the rest of us, it was enough to say that we were there. We can say we saw tennis that had not been seen before and that whatever John Isner and Nicolas Mahut would do for the rest of their lives, nothing would replace the memory of what happened to them on Wimbledon's Court No.18 on Wednesday, June 23, 2010 when they obliterated every record that was ever made.

Could you imagine if Wimbledon followed the policy adopted by the USTA and that five set matches were completed with a tie-break? Isner and Mahut would have gone the way of so many other unheralded, unreported performers who gave their all but were consigned as a result in six-point type at the foot of a page. To play out a fifth set in a Grand Slam tournament is an imperative and what a final set we were privy to.

At 9.10pm, with the light fading, a halt was called to proceedings with the players locked at 59 games all. 59 all!! We had had a 7 hour and 6 minute fifth set up until that moment, a set that had taken longer than the previous longest *match* in the history of the sport, the 6 hours and 33 minutes it had required to separate Frenchmen Fabrice Santoro and Arnaud Clement in the first round of the 2004 Roland Garros. What do they have in the water in France?

Mahut had had to serve 55 times to stay in the match – and there we were a year ago applauding Andy Roddick for having done that 10 times to remain in the final against Roger Federer before he ultimately lost. But 55! "We has to fight like we have never fought before," Mahut said in a snatch interview as the players left the court and made their way wearily to the locker room, a massage and then, to sleep – perchance to dream.

Under normal circumstances, it was a match that would have been granted minimal space, maybe a line in the scores had it not gone on…..and on……and on…..and on. As the score became more and more absurd, giggles broke out from the crowd as Mohamed Lahyani, the umpire, intoned: "Game Isner….Isner leads 43 games to 42 final set… "Game Isner..Isner leads 50 games to 49 final set" etc etc.

What made the match even more compelling was the quality of the serving it provided. What made it unrelenting was that it lacked for anyone able to get anything effective on the other's serve, which could almost have been called dull, depending on your point of view. Isner won points though he could barely move, an effort that was

Nicolas Mahut

beyond words or imagination. As the match entered its ninth hour, Mahut looked as if he could have kept going for another nine.

Physiotherapist, Mark Bender, who looked after the Great Britain Davis Cup team until 2005, described that which Isner and Mahut had achieved – and it was not over yet – as 'incredible' adding 'tennis players are supreme athletes, but even for the sport this was an extraordinary performance. They will be really hurting and going through every kind of pain, because about three hours into the match they would have begun to get cramps, aching backs, shoulders and arms. The concentration required to disregard screaming muscles is huge."

Screaming muscles and minds notwithstanding, when the match was called for the evening (Mahut had said that he was having trouble picking out the yellow balls in the darkening background, which was not evidenced by the way he was playing), Isner rolled his eyes, shrugged and reluctantly stopped. Who knew when this one would ever end?

Just as a taster, by the end of Wednesday evening, the most significant statistics were 192 aces served – Isner led that count 98 to 94 – there had been 163 games played, 118 in the epic fifth set, 877 points played (remarkably 449 to 428 in Mahut's favour), the match had lasted 600 minutes, 6,900 was the number of calories it was suggested each player had burned and finally, one – the number of break points each player had had.

This, said Kevin Mitchell, in *The Guardian*, was "no different to the bare-knuckle pugilists of Georgian myth, no different, either, to something that resides deep in all of us. The question that flickered through most minds of those in attendance and watching on TV was not really who was the better player but what was driving them on? As it turned from absorbing to surreal and continued on towards unbelievable, their struggle took on a life all of its own. Who had seen anything on a sports field to match it for the sheer quality of its weirdness?"

More words had been written about a match that was incomplete than of any of those that separated winner from loser. And there was quite a few of those.➤

On any other day, the fact that Roger Federer lost another set – and almost another – before reaching the third round would have dominated the headlines. As it was, he was now being referred to as, in the word's of the *Daily Mail's* Mike Dickson "Roger, the bullet dodger."

Having almost come a cropper on the opening day, Federer was shifted out to No.1 court where it was assumed to would deal comfortably with Ilija Bozoljac, a Serb who dressed as if heading to some Adriatic sun haven rather than one of the prime tennis courts in the world. As his website kindly informed us, "Ilija's prominence stems more from his eventful love life than his tennis achievements".

Well, for a while, the tennis achievements looked as if they might demand more space, for he was not the slightest bit intimidated by the champion, taking the game to Federer, even after he lost a routine first set. At 4-4 in the second set tie-break, the Swiss showed uncharacteristic panic, hitting a wild forehand that almost landed first bounce into the back fence to offer a mini-break chance that proved decisive.

A sense of normality resumed in the third set but, once more, in the fourth, Bozoljac's initiative was rewarded with three chances to take a 4-2 lead. Federer decided to serve his way out of trouble. The match was completed in a weird way, with both players waiting at the net for the outcome of a Hawk-Eye challenge. "I said to him, I think the ball was out really," Federer said. "He said if it is out, I wish you all the best and please keep on winning. He was very supportive of me going on and playing well. It was an unconventional finish." ➤

Ilija Bozoljac

Speaking of unconventional, who would have thought we would see Amelie Mauresmo coaching a male player at The Championships but here was the 2006 champion in the corner of Michael Llodra, the left hander known for his slapstick personality and slapdash style. Llodra had phoned Mauresmo asking if she felt she might give him a different insight into the preparation for and attitude to trying to win Wimbledon. When she said that she would, it proved to be a fascinating set-up, not least in that Llodra was drawn to be the second round opponent for Roddick, the three-time finalist.

Some took great delight in mocking the Mauresmo-Llodra partnership, suggesting that bringing in a player who had a reputation for losing her way in matches to help with one's psychological outlook was a bit like employing John McEnroe to help with problems of self control. Llodra took it all in good heart. He said he just felt Mauresmo could focus him on the things he needed to focus on and put to the back of his head anything that might cloud his judgement. His victory in the pre-Championship event in Eastbourne suggested they were making a decent fist of it.

Roddick was not taking anyone lightly. Knowing Llodra's talent sharpened the American's instincts and, in the first set, it was the Frenchman who was sharper still, taking the game to Roddick as we sensed he would, not waiting for rallies to develop but trying to break his opponent down by sticking his nose across the net as often as possible. In the opening set, Llodra played flawlessly but he could not quite keep it up. Roddick came out on top 4-6 6-4 6-1 7-6 describing it as "the hardest second round as there would be in this tournament, considering the surface."

One of Roddick's fellow Americans who might have expected a longer stay in the event was Mardy Fish, who had reached the final of the AEGON tournament at Queen's and whose particular brand of quick-fire tennis was well suited. On the other hand, Florian Mayer, of Germany, was a steady-as-you-go kind of player and, on this day, it was unsteady-as-you-go-out for Fish.

The No.7 seed, Nikolay Davydenko, also bit the dust, though this was less surprising. The champion at the 02 Arena in November, when his superior stamina told against a field of relatively tired foes, had only played a single tournament since March when suffering from wrist problems and had almost been knocked out in the first round by a giant figure serving bombs. Confronting a second in succession was too much, Davydenko losing 1-6 7-6 7-6 6-1 to Daniel Brands, an enterprising player from Germany.

In the women's event, Justine Henin, of Belgium, was slowly finding her feet, after four years away from grass. She defeated another German, Kristina Barrois, in straight sets, though the closeness of the result, 6-3 7-5, had more to do with Henin idling in front, like a dodgy racehorse.

Andy Roddick

"I've had a couple of those experiences like Younes El Aynaoui way back when (the 21-19 quarter final of the 2003 Australian Open). You've got to harp on those first points of every service game, try to get those. Love-15, 15-30, that starts becoming dicey. Beyond that, you just have to try to convince yourself that it's only going to be another 10 or 15 minutes out there, even if you might not believe it at the time".

At her best, Henin still danced into her game, with a single-handed backhand selected by John McEnroe – who had no mean single-hander himself – as the best in the women's game (as well as the men's). She had an athletic, all court game and remained the best you will see at turning defence into attack. And remember volleys – the shot they used to play on grass? Henin went to the net 29 times and won the point 21 times, indicative of a different, slightly more aggressive approach to the game. Not that she regarded herself as one of the favourites. "I see myself as an outsider," she insisted. Others begged to differ.

There were a couple of upsets on the women's side, notably the loss of Shahar Peer, the No.13 seed from Israel who was beaten 3-6 6-3 6-4 by Angelique Kerber, of Germany, and Melanie Oudin, the American, who had struggled to live up to the notoriety she had gained at last year's US Open, losing 6-4 6-3 to Australia's Jarmila Groth.

While all of this was happening, Isner and Mahut were still hard at it. Words began to fail you.

Justine Henin v Kristina Barrois

49

Thursday June 24…

We were all craning our necks. I was standing between Andy Murray's grandparents, Roy and Shirley, on the players' lawn, hoping this was a vantage point where we could best see what was going on. No, no, silly, not whether John Isner or Nicolas Mahut would prevail in the match of a generation, but what she looked like. You know who I mean, the lady who had not been here for 33 years and had all of the All England Club in a right royal tizz.

Everyone was where they ought to have been but we had been told to expect the personage in question at just gone 11am and here it was at 11.20 and still no sign. She had not changed her mind, surely. Imagine all those practice curtseys and bows coming to nothing. Roger Federer arrived looking smarter than one had ever seen him, in club purple and green tie and the most pristine white shirt he had ever worn on the premises. Mirka, his wife, looked absolutely divine.

How utterly radiant she looked. What was the colour of her outfit? Turquoise? Powder Blue? Eau de Nil? The women would have a field day debating that one. She disappeared from sight, to re-appear a couple of minutes later (we had to watch television to see her this time) on the Member's Lawn to be greeted by a phalanx of players looking very shiny indeed. Andy Roddick's cream jacket took the biscuit; Serena Williams' curtsey was as extravagant as she had promised it would be. Luckily, she did not ask Novak Djokovic to do his impersonations.

As she crossed the bridge from the Members' into Centre Court, the reception afforded her was rapturous, as was only right. Tim Phillips, in his last year as chairman, had every reason to look extremely chuffed. Off they went to dine on Orange and Honey Marinated Chicken on Fruity Couscous with Roasted Vegetables; followed by Kentish Strawberries and Blackberries with Cornish Clotted Cream and Mint Syrup, all washed down with the finest Meursault and Barolo. Someone, and I cannot possibly divulge who, revealed to me that the Queen did not leave a morsel, so that was a major victory for the caterers.

Her Majesty The Queen meets Roger Federer, Serena Wlliams and Novak Djokovic (top photo) and Billie-Jean King and Laura Robson

Then there was a frisson on Henman Hill, a smattering of applause we could just about hear from where we were at the far end of St Mary's Walk. She was just distinguishable now. Well, we could see the hat. There was an awful lot of commotion, plenty of people who looked terribly important were there. The figure approached but then took a detour, onto Court No.14. But weren't Isner and Mahut re-starting again on 18 where it had all gone off before?

Then we could see Her Majesty The Queen.

**Andy Murray and Jarkko Nieminen bow to
The Queen**

There was still tennis being played, but we had been diverted. An hour drifted by and, as Centre Court buzzed with anticipation, there were three seats left to be filled in the Royal Box, the chairman, the honorary president, the Duke of Kent and the patron, The Queen. The crowd rose as one to greet her. She proffered two waves in response. We all settled back.

Murray and Jarkko Nieminen, of Finland, were to be the final dish to set before Her Majesty. On the pair came, turned, placed their racket bags neatly at their feet and, with right arm across tummy and left arm neatly behind back, they bowed as decent a pair of bows as one had ever seen. Simon Barnes, in *The Times*, witnessed it and revealed. "He (Murray) bowed so neatly and pedantically as if anxious to get it just right to leave no one an atom of opportunity to criticise him for latent republicanism, disrespect, Scottishness or any other terrible sin.

"Nieminen grovelled. He left not an atom of opportunity to doubt Murray's complete dominance over three sets of tennis (they're like chukkas, Ma'am, only different). Murray won 6-3 6-4 6-2. The Queen was paying her first visit to Wimbledon since 1977, her Silver Jubilee year in which Virginia Wade was crowned queen of SW19. Obviously, this makes the royal visit an incontrovertible omen for the coronation of Murray. And one's subject did jolly well yesterday".

Andy Murray

It pleased everyone, not least Murray himself, that the match was completed in double quick time, an hour and 43 minutes to be exact. An opening service game in which he had to save four break points – serving with one's back to the monarch must be terribly difficult – he completed with an ace, broke Nieminen immediately and was on his way to a compelling success, one break in the second, two further in the third and we were back to the bows again.

There was a couple more on the members' balcony as Murray and Nieminen were introduced personally to The Queen. "A private conversation," the Scot said when he was asked what had been said. Nieminen was a little more revealing, suggesting that he had been told that The Queen was particularly impressed with the way he moved across the court.

Before Caroline Wozniacki and Kai-Chen Chang, of Taiwan, had made their way out to play next, the royal party was on its way out of the grounds, sufficiently sated. The sweat stains that had begun to form on certain collars ran dry. We could all breathe again.

Jarkko Nieminen and Andy Murray meet The Queen after their match

John Isner, Nicolas Mahut and umpire, Mohamed Lahyani

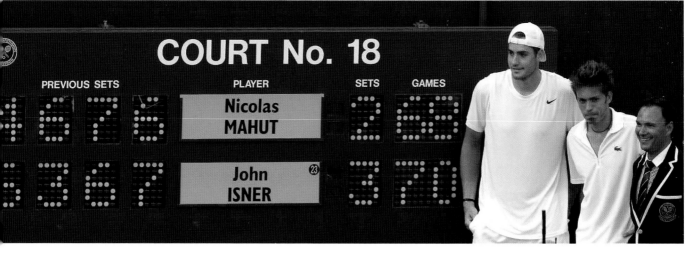

Not before 3.30pm were Isner and Mahut to re-engage. That should have been enough time to shake some life back into their bodies. Andy Roddick had brought Isner a pizza, chicken and mashed potatoes for his dinner. He had had four hours sleep. For 65 minutes more they were to do battle, finally parted when, at 69-68 to the American, the opportunity presented itself when his backhand service return drew Mahut forward to play a half volley which sat up nicely. Even as he saw its trajectory, the Frenchman must have feared the worst and a backhand pass fizzed past him, at which Isner threw himself backwards, getting up pretty quickly, fearing that if he stayed down too long all his joints would seize.

Mahut's effort earned him £16.92 a minute – chicken feed. Since the match had started, 85 other matches had been completed over the course of The Championships; Greece, Nigeria, Slovenia, Algeria, Australia and Serbia were knocked out of the World Cup; Australia had a new Prime Minister, Julia Gillard, the first woman PM there; General Stanley McChrystal had been fired as US and NATO commander in Afghanistan and the British coalition government had unveiled plans to make men wait an extra year before receiving their pension. It seemed to me that one had aged that year in three days anyway.

Mahut was devastated, almost inconsolable. We tried to wrap him up in the historical perspective but all that seemed to matter to him was that he had lost. "This is just a match I will never forget. I hope the people who watched the match will say the same. At this moment, though, it is really painful," he said. "I lost this match. I just wanted to win. He was just better than me. Tonight it is very difficult to talk about it." It would have taken a hard man not to feel for Mahut at this time, a genuine nice man, a fine player, whose name was now in folklore but, to his mind, for the wrong reasons.

The score, for the pedants, was 6-4 3-6 6-7 7-6 70-68. At the end of proceedings, Mahut simply wanted to walk away but was made to stand for a picture at the scoreboard (he was the decidedly glum one in the middle) and receive a crystal bowl which, one hoped for the engraver's sake, was not shattered the minute he returned to the locker room.

Ed Smith, the former England batsman, and now a leader writer for *The Times*, had some fascinating words on the subject. "We kid ourselves that sport is all about winning, about being the best, about quantifiable supremacy. It isn't. The phrase 'winning is the only thing that matters' is both depressing and wrong. Sport inspires us most when it taps into timeless human narratives. In yesterday's final act, one of them had to lose. But, by then, both had won something much bigger than a tennis match. They found out what they were capable of, how deep were their reserves of resilience and willpower. That is the ultimate prize in sport. And we should applaud it to the rafters when we see it". ➤

At last! John Isner after his victory over Nicolas Mahut

Rafael Nadal

And so to other things. Rafael Nadal was on Centre Court against Robin Haase, of The Netherlands, a player who would certainly have bettered his career high ranking of No.56 (in mid-2008) by now had he not suffered serious problems with his knees in the past two years. Nadal knew what that was like! Haase was currently at a modest No.151 but on the rise again. Nadal knew he would be in for a tough time, but perhaps not quite this tough.

Haase's first serve was fast, accurate and, at times, too hot for the Spaniard to handle. It was likened, by Ivan Speck, in the *Daily Mail*, to "Twenty20 tennis, quick-fire and bursting with life; a flamethrower of a match with winners singeing every inch of the court. Five sets in two hours and 22 minutes, classic early evening Wimbledon fare".

Nadal won it 5-7 6-2 3-6 6-0 6-3 and only did so because, in the final set, he buckled down and got the basic rights whereas Haase was still throwing himself into drive volleys which would, ultimately, not come off later in the match as wondrously as they had early on.

The Swedish journalists, who far outnumbered their lone participant in the men's singles, Robin Soderling, were not entirely confident about their

Robin Haase

man's chances against Spain's Marcel Granollers, who had taken Soderling to four sets in the second round of last year's Championships and beaten him in five in the first of this year's Australian Open. Sometimes one player did not match up well against another, and nobody quite knew why. There was a collective sigh of relief when Soderling came through – a bit edgily in the first set – 7-5 6-1 6-4.

Out on Court No.2, we found Serena Williams. Better not to ask her what she thought about it, because she had been practising her curtsey for days, but obviously the order of play rankled with the defending champion so much that she decided to take out her angst on Anna Chakvetadze, a Russian, who had been ranked inside the top ten in 2007 but was now at No.118. Such statistical niceties meant nothing to Serena – five second-serve aces rather underlining her mood.

The day's festivities almost ended with the world No.1 men's doubles pair and defending champion losing their place in the event. Daniel Nestor and Nenad Zimonjic were facing Britain's Jamie Murray and Jonny Marray on the court that is slap-bang in front of the member's balcony and there was plenty of tea spilling into saucers as Jonny and Jamie thrashed the ball to some effect before going down 6-3 6-7 7-6 6-7 15-13.

QUOTES of the Day
NICOLAS MAHUT:

"I didn't sleep so much (on Wednesday night). Like three hours or something. I had a massage, I took a cold bath. I ate some pasta or something but I wasn't hungry. I just wanted to play today. I was waiting. I was just waiting for the match. I just wanted to win. It's really painful to lose this kind of match."

QUOTES of the Day
JOHN ISNER:

"After a certain point, maybe 25-all, I lost track of the score. I was just going there, holding serve, walking to the bench deliriously, getting up and not breaking, then holding. I did that for seven hours really. Yeah, I forgot about the score."

John Isner

Friday 25 June...

There was a sense that we could all do with a day that was a little quieter. Bleary-eyed and full of wonder after the events of Thursday, a return to normality was required as Friday dawned, blissfully sun-kissed as the first four days had been. Until darkness started to fall, that was exactly what we had.

As we started to lull into Day Five though, the dreamy mood was interrupted by Philippe Bouin,

doyen of French writers who approached me brandishing a set of papers on which the score of the John Isner-Nicolas Mahut epic was printed. Philippe had noticed a couple of discrepancies and because the match mattered more to the French than anyone else, this stickler for right and wrong wanted to know the score (literally).

On one piece of paper, the time of the match was set at 11 hours and 5 minutes, on another, it was 11 hours and 8. It was subsequently discovered that

QUOTE of the Day

QUESTION TO JOHN ISNER:

"Were you at any stage jealous of an opponent (Thiemo De Bakker) whose final set in the last round was 16-14, to your 70-68?"

ANSWER:

"Yeah, I was. And yesterday he didn't play at all. I'd still rather be in his position, in the third round. It stinks to lose in the second round."

the three minutes which had been spent in debate at the end of the night on Wednesday about the dimness of the light and whether the match should be suspended had been included in the time of the fifth set. (Bouin also discovered in 15 other instances the statistics from the umpire's scorecard and the official timekeepers at IBM did not match, provoking much deliberation behind the scenes).

We should briefly mention Isner once more. As he made his way towards No.5 Court, the

American received a rousing reception but it was plodding progress, there was little life in his body and when he tried to serve against Thiemo De Bakker, of The Netherlands, he could barely manage something that had come so destructively easy to him the previous three days.

As such, Isner fell 6-0 6-3 6-2 to the Dutchman whose coach, Matt Merkel, was delighted at how De Bakker retained his focus and refused to let the occasion worry him. "Had Thiemo given the   ➢

slightest indication that he would relax, John might have seized on it and got a new lease of life, but he didn't," Merkel (no relation to the German Chancellor) said. "It was very impressive". Isner was bidden a fond farewell. The Championships, the sport, would not forget him.

Nor would it Mahut who, by the by, had been forced to start a doubles match on Thursday night with his partner, Arnaud Clement – "He was still hopping about, that guy has to be the Energizer Bunny", Isner said – which was completed with the defeat that had to have been expected to the British pair, Colin Fleming and Ken Skupski.

Talking of Energizer bunnies, Lleyton Hewitt was still in the competition. Indeed, the 28-year-old Australian had won his 28th title the week before The Championships, turning over Roger Federer in the final of the Gerry Weber Open in Halle, Germany. It was only the second time in eight years that the Swiss had lost a match on grass – the other being in a certain final somewhere very close in 2008.

As one watched Liam Broady, a British junior hitting with Rafael Nadal at Aorangi Park, where the ball seemed to be coming pretty powerfully from his strings, one's mind turned to kids with

attitude. When asked the previous week to nominate the young British player who most epitomised the attitude required to succeed, Andy Murray had said Broady, from Stockport.

Broady bore an uncanny resemblance to a teenage Hewitt, the blond hair, cap worn backwards and a look in his eye that suggested he was going to make the most of his desire to become a successful player. That he was born in the same town as Fred Perry added a certain piquancy to the story, as did the fact that his family did not conform to the strictures preferred by the British tennis hierarchy. Remind you of someone?

Hewitt had never been a conformist. He had reached this stage of his career by staying loyal to his reactionary roots, a tough-as-old-boots kid whose parents brooked no argument and who still played each match as if life itself depended on the outcome. He set the folk of Tennis Australia on edge but where would tennis in Australia have been without him to keep it in the nation's mind's eye this past decade?

On Centre Court, Hewitt's 6-3 7-6 6-4 victory over Gael Monfils, of France, defined the 2002 champion's refusal to let one of the sport's more

Lleyton Hewitt

Roger Federer

volatile characters break the levels of
concentration and intensity that had been his
hallmarks. For two sets, Hewitt served out of his
skin, dropping a mere six points before the second
set tie-break, from which he extricated himself
after three feeble netted forehands. The
Frenchman then became ragged himself and
Hewitt took the set with a delightful backhand
volley that tested his dodgy hips to the utmost.

Before this year's Australian Open, where he
lost in the fourth round to Roger Federer, Hewitt
knew he would have to go into hospital for a
second hip operation, something he kept from all
but his nearest and dearest which was typical of
the man. He had not lasted more than a couple of
rounds at any event until the French Open when
he took ten sets in three games from Nadal, a
decent effort.

Roger Rasheed, who coached Hewitt for three
years before a falling out led to him moving on to
take care of Monfils, had known this match would
be tough. He said that the minute his former
charge walked back through the gates of SW19, he
was 'like a kid in a candy store.' It was a little too
easy to help himself from the top shelf this day.

The same was true of Federer who followed
Hewitt onto Centre. If he could have hand-picked
an opponent to play at the end of an unusually
testing first week, who better than the 32-year-old
Clement? Within three games, it was obvious to
Federer – and 15,000 witnesses – he was going to
win and the matter of interest seemed to be how
long it would take him. An hour and 35 minutes
was your answer.

➤

"The match in the last round (against Ilija Bozoljac) was hard to judge because there was just serving, bombing, returning, reacting," he said. "In the first match I was in trouble for four sets and only in the fifth could I start playing some normal tennis. So today, obviously, I felt much better. Right off the bat, I got an early break. Same thing in the second and from then on, it was a race to the finish line. It was a good and solid match for me, clean, hardly any errors, good on the offensive. I'm very happy with my game right now."

And few days had been as agreeable of late for Novak Djokovic as the one he experienced against Albert Montanes, of Spain, especially for a player who had tended to wilt in these stifling conditions before. As Julian Muscat, in *The Times*,

Novak Djokovic

said, "Novak's erratic serve was on its best behaviour and, in Montanes, he was tossed a most obliging opponent."

At 5-4, when Djokovic was serving for the second set, we had a demonstration of Montanes' culpability. The Serbian should have been feeling invincible for he had dropped only eight points in as many previous service games, yet his first delivery was so wild that only Hawk-Eye knew whether the ball had struck the baseline or bounced beyond it. Djokovic was rendered so rigid that he promptly double-faulted.

Here was Montanes' chance. Djokovic played the next point nervously, offering his opponent a half-court ball that he ought to have brushed for love-30. But the hapless Spaniard found the net, in the process allowing the No.3 seed to rediscover the equilibrium that had momentarily deserted him. On such moments, could matches often be determined. "I am always self-critical," Djokovic said. "I haven't been at my best for the past five months but I have been managing to hold on."

Of the matches one had earmarked as requiring special attention this day, Romania's Victor Hanescu against Daniel Brands, of Germany, two unseeded giants, was not one. You cannot be everywhere all the time and No.18 Court had been ➤

the centre of attention for three days and perhaps one should have expected the unexpected. That evening would occur the one and only explicitly unsavoury incident of the tournament. Briefly, Hanescu had reached two sets all when he asked the umpire for a ruling on the fading light, at the same time as complaining of a hamstring injury.

The ruling that the match should continue clearly irked Hanescu whose lack of interest in proceedings fed to the crowd which began to barrack him. Hanescu, who has spent his entire career avoiding controversy – indeed he was once said to 'have Bjorn Borg's temperament but not the results' – relieved himself of some phlegm in the direction of spectators for which he was given a warning for unsportsmanlike conduct. With that, so those at courtside suggested, he began to foot fault deliberately and, at 3-0 down in the final set, shook hands with a bemused Brands.

A review of television tapes was demanded by Andrew Jarrett, the referee, after which he announced, "Victor Hanescu has been fined $7,500 (£5,000) for unsportsmanlike conduct and a further $7,500 (£5,000) for not using best efforts at the conclusion of the match. No further comment will be made by the referee or the chair umpire". Four spectators were arrested after the match for 'behaviour likely to cause harassment, alarm or distress'. They were later released.

Back where it mattered, Jelena Jankovic, the No.4 seed, was making her way stealthily into the last 16, defeating Alona Bondarenko, of Ukraine, for the loss of only three games. The first set lasted 14 minutes, which was head-shakingly quick. Before the hour was up – and that included a 10-minute delay while Jankovic received her obligatory injury time-out – she had won 6-0 6-3 and the long lunchers had missed her.

Another player at the opposite end of the Isner scale, Marion Bartoli, the 2007 runner up from France, was dispensing with Greta Arn, of Hungary, 6-3 6-4 and could quite rightly have been said to have enjoyed a dream first week, winning a first round in 80 minutes, having had her second round opponent withdraw before a ball was struck, taking quick care of Arn and not having to face Francesca Schiavone, the French Open champion at all, after she had disappeared from her section by mid-afternoon on the opening day.

"I think I will pretty much have a chance of making the final every year I play this tournament," Bartoli said. With the kind of fortune that had smiled on her in week one, why not?

Marion Bartoli

Day **SIX**
26.06.2010

PETZSCHNER
vs
NADAL

SIMON
vs
MURRAY

MALISSE
vs
QUERREY

S. WILLIAMS
vs
CIBULKOVA

NESTOR AND ZIMONJIC
vs
EATON AND INGLOT

Saturday 26 June…

**What had been his game plan, Philipp
Petzschner, of Germany, was asked in the
aftermath of the match that was to rank
third in the opening week full of "Did I
Really See That, Or Was It A Figment Of
My Imagination?" episodes. Petzschner had
lost in five sets to Rafael Nadal on Centre
Court. "Play Crazy" was his response. And
play crazy he did.**

We had become so used to the crazies as part and
parcel of the 2010 Championships that had Nadal
beaten his retreat, few would have been totally
surprised. For the second time in successive rounds,
the Spaniard had been two sets to one down and not
any old where, but the court on which he had enjoyed
the most satisfying moment of his career.

Petzschner had been picked out as a possible fly
in the ointment for he was not one of the more
regular players we see week in and week out on
the tour, he was someone with an intuitive
flamboyance, who preferred to make opponents
have to play a winner than sit back and wait for
their pounding ground strokes to take effect. It was
clear that he had the right ideas to infuriate Nadal
but did he have the sustained strength in body and
soul to see it through?

The answer was 'Nein' but he gave it a
resoundingly good go. Nadal eventually emerged
6-4 4-6 6-7 6-2 6-3 and the debate afterwards had
more to do with injury time-outs, cranky knees and
crankier umpires than it did about the levels of
tennis. That was sometimes the way of things.

Cedric Mourier, of France, a well respected man
in the chair, called Nadal for coaching at one stage
in the match. Now Nadal is not a man given to on-
court demonstrations; indeed he has never thrown a
strop or a racket to the ground in his life, but this
decision did not go down at all well. The Spanish
writers thought he may have let fly a naughty word
but on closer inspection Nadal had simply said to
Mourier "we're going to talk to the supervisor
later". It was as close to a rage as he got.

Nadal was not moving as well as one would have
expected, and Petzschner, who had by no means
been brilliant in the first two sets, started to attack,
open his shoulders and hit a succession of forehand
winners. Come the third set tie-break, Nadal won
the first two points, but after that the German was
in command, finishing it off with another searing
ace. Towards the end of that set, Nadal had
requested the attendance of the trainer. But, after
the tie-break, he sent him away.   ➤

To acknowledge Armed Forces Day, invited military personnel were given a standing ovation

Nick Pitt, of *The Sunday Times,* takes up the story, "Three games into the fourth set, Nadal called the trainer again and received treatment to his right knee and thigh. Petzschner did not seem pleased to have his momentum broken, particularly since Nadal had not shown obvious signs of discomfort. He had just been flat and out of sorts. The treatment, or the break, did wonders for Nadal. He moved better and began to play more aggressively, taking to the forecourt to force Petzschner to snatch at his shots.

"Both men were suffering physically in the fifth. Petzschner, who went five sets in both his previous matches, and had also been playing men's doubles and mixed doubles, was running on empty. Nadal did not seem so tired, but he was hampered in his movement, forcing himself to run down balls when it must have hurt him to do so. The fight was intense, and when Nadal was warned for getting coaching advice from his uncle in the stands, it enraged and energised him".

Enough to land his expected spot in the fourth round and to confess he had already taken the decision not to play the Davis Cup World Group quarter-final against France the weekend after The Championships, requiring a period of rest, however deep into the event he might go.

How we hoped it would be some way yet. Nadal had a special place in many hearts, not least with fellow sportsmen who had more idea than any about what it was that made him so special. On the middle Saturday, as per tradition, a large number

of the Centre Court seats were occupied by such sportsmen: Sir Chris Hoy, Sir Bobby Charlton, Dame Kelly Holmes, Glenn Hoddle, Lewis Moody, Jason Leonard, Sachin Tendulkar and Brian Lara to name a goodly few.

This was Armed Forces Day and, by means of recognition for the selfless service given by these brave people, it had been decided that 14 servicemen and women from each of the three services had been invited to sit in on Saturday. The troops had all recently returned from operations around the world. They looked inspiring as was the standing ovation that greeted them.

Over 300 personnel from the services attend The Championships each year to act as stewards on the three show courts. Leading Seaman Stuart Linnahan joined the Royal Navy in 1995 and was deployed to Iraq with its training team in 2004. He said, "It was only a year after the war and everything was still a bit tetchy, but the Iraqi people really wanted to learn about how to do it themselves so we could quietly start moving out of Iraq. That was a great high for me as I was doing my job and giving something back to people.

"Being here at Wimbledon, when you're in uniform the public gets to see you. Over the past 15 years, whether there have been highs or lows, people can see me and I can know that they are seeing the Royal Navy through me. So Wimbledon for me is a bit of tennis, but it's also a chance for me to stand there and let the public see me." ➤

As much as any of us, the soldiers, sailors and air force crews wondered whether they might witness a little bit of British battling all the way to the Wimbledon final. Exhibitionist shows of egotism were not Andy Murray's style: two years had passed since that famous Centre Court flex of a bulging bicep and, more recently, he decided the Ferrari he had purchased for himself was too pretentious a means of transport.

However, place Britain's lone tennis star in front of a group of sporting icons and fighters that he reveres at Wimbledon and the heroics will follow. Sir Chris Hoy had made a point of being in Murray's corner when his compatriot played the final of the Australian Open and came up short against Roger Federer. Home territory, and

admittedly a distinctly less exacting opponent in Gilles Simon, meant Scotland's most accomplished sportsman left not only celebrating an emphatic victory by his countryman but brimful of hope that greater things are to follow.

Three rounds accomplished in straight sets and a service that had held firm since the opening exchanges of Murray's first-round match; it could not get much more satisfying than that, and the No.4 seed relished a 6-1 6-4 6-4 victory over Simon, which was as close to faultless as the 23-year-old has been since Marin Cilic fell to him in the Australian semi-final.

"I'm going to have to play a lot better next week if I want to go all the way. It's kind of tough to compare the two tournaments," Murray, not

Andy Murray

wishing to be drawn into the trap of assuming another path to a final is opening up before him, said. "However, in terms of the way this first week's gone, it's been great. Now I've got to try and build on that".

Murray would now play Sam Querrey, of the United States, the man who had replaced him as the AEGON champion at Queen's Club two weekends earlier. Querrey and Xavier Malisse, of Belgium, had been locked in a five-set match every bit as fascinating as that between Nadal and Petzschner; indeed it appeared as if they may have to return to the court on Monday as the fifth set dragged on (and wouldn't you know it, the chair umpire was Mohamed Lahyani, of Isner/Mahut fame!).

"It was pretty much dark in the last game," Querrey admitted. "I think if he had broken me for 8-all, we would have had to stop then. We would have had to think about it for a full day. It was getting rather tough to see out there but the umpire didn't say anything. If he had said 'all right, last game' it might make it unfair if you're the one serving." Querrey held on. Just.

The remarkable element about the eight women's singles matches played on the middle Saturday, was that not a single one of them was extended beyond two sets. It was almost as if they did not want to hog the courts for too long. There were two love sets, one not such a shock, one something of a stunner.

Gilles Simon

Dominika Cibulkova

Petra Kvitova

Klara Zakopalova

Serena Williams, as was her wont, steamrollered through a first set against Dominika Cibulkova, of Slovakia, before her challenger threw Centre Court stage fright to one side and made the second set a much more watchable 7-5. Out on Court No.18 (not there again!), Victoria Azarenka, of Belarus, the No.14 seed, might have been expected to have strengthened her sinews after losing the opening set to Petra Kvitova of the Czech Republic – instead of which she subsided 6-0 in the second. The tenth seed, Flavia Pennetta, of Italy, was also dispatched without much ado, losing 6-2 6-3 to Klara Zakopalova, also of the Czech Republic.

A hubbub was growing around Court No.6, the mid-point of the stretch of courts in front of the members' balcony. Daniel Nestor and Nenad Zimonjic, the defending champions, having seen off Jamie Murray and Jonny Marray 15-13 in the final set in the first round, were now locking horns with another British pair, Chris Eaton and Dominic Inglot, in the second.

Eaton had been the new face of the game two years earlier when he qualified for The Championships and won a round – remember the guy with the battered Vauxhall who got all those marriage proposals? Well, he had not moved on

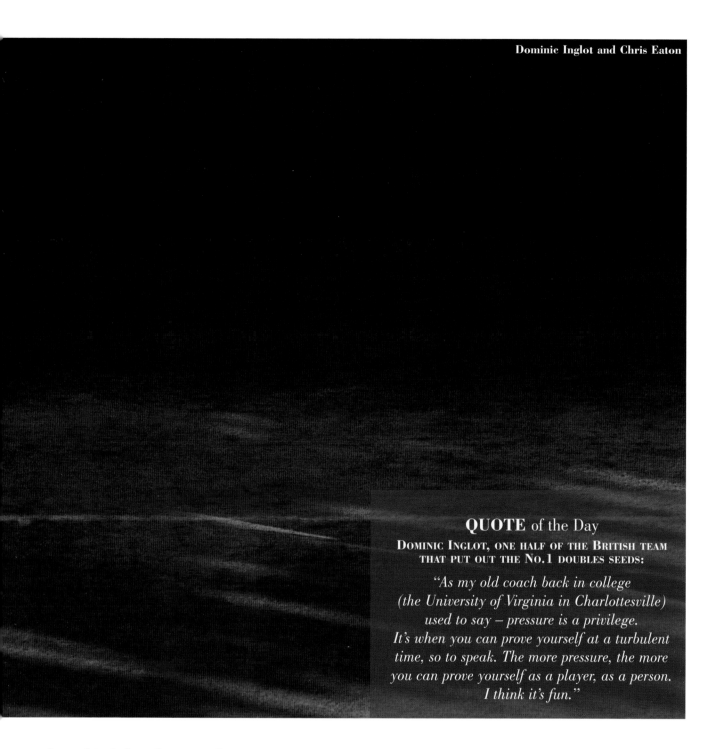

QUOTE of the Day

DOMINIC INGLOT, ONE HALF OF THE BRITISH TEAM
THAT PUT OUT THE NO.1 DOUBLES SEEDS:

*"As my old coach back in college
(the University of Virginia in Charlottesville)
used to say – pressure is a privilege.
It's when you can prove yourself at a turbulent
time, so to speak. The more pressure, the more
you can prove yourself as a player, as a person.
I think it's fun."*

that much in singles in the meantime but was
playing a mean game of doubles with Inglot, his
heavy-serving pal. They thundered around,
leaping, laughing, loving every minute of it and
against grim-faced opponents who were not exactly
happy to have been sentenced to the hinterland
again (what was it with purely doubles players
thinking they had a right to be scheduled on
Centre or No.1 until the final?), had the greater
will to win. They did so, 7-5 5-7 7-6 6-7 8-6.
Very nice it was, too.

Day **SEVEN**
28.06.2010

FEDERER
VS
MELTZER

MURRAY
VS
QUERREY

RODDICK
VS
LU

SODERLING
VS
FERRER

V. WILLIAMS
VS
GROTH

HENIN
VS
CLIJSTERS

S. WILLIAMS
VS
SHARAPOVA

Monday 28 June…

Elsewhere, folk were getting all het up about a ball that hit the underside of a crossbar, bounced down a yard over the line and, theoretically, cost England a place in the last eight of the World Cup. The demands back home were – in no procedural order – for the coach's head, the instant flogging of the entire squad, the immediate introduction of goal-line technology and anything else we could think of to assuage our collective grief. Anyway, it meant that Frank Lampard, striker of said ball, could be home in time to attend the 25-year celebration of Boris Becker's 1985 Wimbledon triumph, so all was not entirely lost.

Roger Federer, who had never been converted to the need for the Hawk-Eye electronic line calling system in his own sport, had some sympathy with the suggestion that it should be brought into football, though he may have been mindful of which country he was in when the subject was raised with him. Also, he said, was not the man in charge – FIFA president, Sepp Blatter – a Swiss? He could not condemn totally then.

Poor Andy Murray, he knew it was coming, too. As soon as England was dispatched from the competition, so inevitably those eyes and lenses that had been trained on what was happening in South Africa, would turn back to SW19. All he could do was to carry on as if nothing else tumultuous in sport had happened, and fourth round day at The Championships always carried with it a special sense of occasion few other sporting galas could match.

There were eight men's and eight women's singles to be played, a nightmare for the Order of Play committee to determine which of the remainder of the field would be sent to the club's hinterland. Justine Henin had played Kim Clijsters, her fellow countrywoman, in three Grand Slam tournament finals – as well as three further semi-finals and a quarter-final – and the matches had always been staged on the premier court. Not this time. Serena Williams against Maria Sharapova was regarded as slightly more box office.

A lot of people thought that Novak Djokovic against Lleyton Hewitt was a better match than Federer against Jurgen Melzer, even though the Austrian had recently reached the French Open semi-finals. Federer got to return to Centre, whereas Djokovic, Hewitt, Rafael Nadal, Henin and Clijsters, were sent to No.1 Court. Boy, what a day to have a ticket there.

Federer took care of Melzer 6-3 6-2 6-3, about as comfortable a passage as he could possibly have anticipated. He was asked about the hot and dry weather and said he regarded it as moderate "a one-shirt-change kind of match". Talk about self-control. While the rest of the tournament – and the world it seemed – were getting all hot under the collar, the Swiss champion was the personification of cool.

This was, after all, the time to declare one's hand. The second week meant the start of the real business of the tournament. "Show us what you're made of, Roger," a lone voice called from the gallery. Well, at times, he was quite unplayable, it was as if he had settled down to a lobster lunch, using every implement to crack, crush and fillet out every last morsel. Melzer was the empty shell on his plate – and that after Federer had swallowed the starter whole. The Austrian opened with six successive errors, only one of them forced from him. The match was as good as sorted.

The second men's match on Centre pitted Andy Murray and Sam Querrey, the last two winners of the Queen's Club title, bravado against big serve, brains versus brawn. Brian Viner, of *The Independent*, chose to watch it unfold from Henman Hill, surrounded, as he said, by more red necks than a Baton Rouge trailer park.

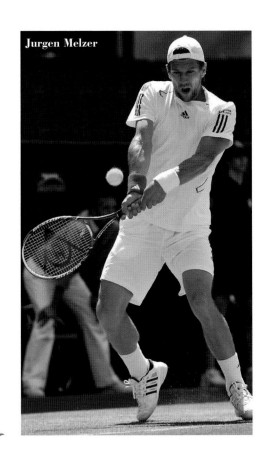

Jurgen Melzer

Roger Federer

"Judging by the state of one bad man in an England football shirt snoring gently through Murray v. Querrey, every part of the warning to 'drink plenty of water, wear a hat and apply sunscreen' had been roundly ignored. He was by no means the only one enjoying a snooze though, and on the steepest bits of the slope this wasn't an altogether good idea, since the combination of human traffic and warm sunshine had rendered it slippery. More than one sleeping form spent the late afternoon edging slowly, but perceptibly, downhill."

Murray, to the relief of everyone in the grounds not from California, was able to negotiate Querrey 7-5 6-3 6-4, maintaining his not-a-set-relinquishing form. In essence, the match boiled down to two games. The first was the eleventh of the first set. Murray had allowed three set points to drift from his grasp in the ninth, Querrey held for 5-5 and three points went by in a blur of Murray errors and miscalculations. It was here that his pig-headedness kicked in.

Sam Querrey

Andy Murray

Lu. Who? Lu! There did seem to be only one way to defeat Andy Roddick at the All England Club recently and that was deep into a fifth set. Last year, in the final, he lost 16-14 at the stage and the world had a lump in its throat for him; on this day it was to be 9-7 to the world No.82, who broke the American's serve just once in four hours and 36 minutes. In doing so, he broke his heart. ➤

Yen-Hsun Lu

He saved the first break point with a forehand winner, the second with a regal backhand and Querrey, over anxious, took too much of a swing at a forehand, one of his finer shots, on the third. It was as if someone had whispered in the American's ear that this was not going to be his day.

The second key game was the penultimate of the match and one that was worth the £70 admission fee. It was 4-4, with Querrey serving and Murray in one of his on-court trances, sticking superbly in the rallies, slicing and dicing and, at 30-all, making tracks to a crosscourt volley from his opponent and contriving a remarkable backhand scoop down the line. Judy, his mother, was on her feet before the ball had landed, so many times had she seen her son make that shot. Very soon, the match was over.

Joining Federer and Murray in the quarter-finals were Nadal, Djokovic, Robin Soderling, Jo-Wilfried Tsonga, Tomas Berdych and Yen-Hsun

Novak
Djokovic

Roddick's eyes were hollow and haunted in the press conference later, "He deserved to win more than I did, that's for sure," the man who had set such stall on the event, said. "It wasn't my serve, it was my returning. It was cr*p. Through three sets, I was playing horrendously and I actually think the fifth was the best I played as far as making him struggle but, when you dig yourself a hole, it's tough to get out."

Lu would now play Djokovic, who having won the first two sets against Lleyton Hewitt, demanded a medical time-out. We feared he was having trouble breathing, that he may have been suffering another of the anxiety attacks that overcame him at critical moments, but it was discovered from his coaching set-up later that he needed to take something for a bout of indigestion, nothing more serious than that. Djokovic celebrated by ripping open his shirt, tearing it off and hurling it into the crowd, Pat Rafter-like. He may have had a dodgy stomach but his biceps were clearly functioning. Hewitt did not much like any of it. "He's always got something," the Australian muttered later.

Perhaps the match of the day on the men's side was on Court No.12, where Soderling, the French Open finalist, had been sent. His opponent was David Ferrer, a Spaniard, who had never become quite as attached to Wimbledon as Nadal or Juan ➤

Andy Roddick

Robin Soderling

Carlos Ferrero, but who was scampering around as ever, making opponents draw on every last fine shot to beat him. Ferrer was dogged, really dogged, but so too was Soderling who triumphed 6-2 5-7 6-2 3-6 7-5 in three hours.

Speaking of those who had to find their way to the Wimbledon outreaches, Venus Williams negotiated her way into the last eight more efficiently than she found No.2 Court. This was the five-time champion's bow out there but when the call came for the noon start came and went and the locker room emptied, Venus was still sitting there. Had she not kicked up a fuss, and another five minutes gone by, she could have been defaulted.

Unaware of her plight, she was greeted at 12.10pm with a few jeers, and if the crowd was roused in their support of Jarmila Groth, the Australian who was able to play the game with the racket in either hand but slightly favoured her right, it was not enough to see her over the challenge of Williams, who won 6-4 7-6.

The Belgian journalists were all of a flutter on No.1. The overwhelming majority of them considered Henin would be too strong for Clijsters. They were wrong. *The Times'* Europe correspondent, David Charter, had written about

Belgium being "deeply divided, but hoping to present a united face to the world. It was a country split along language lines and facing an existential crisis. After the success of a Flemish separatist party in the recent general election, calls had intensified for a Czechoslovak-style divorce of the country." And we thought this was sport.

Away from political wrangling (and Henin was from the Francophone south and Clijsters from the Flemish-speaking northern region of Flanders) there was tennis to be played and how well they played it. Both had re-acquainted themselves with grass after a long period away, Clijsters to start a family, Henin to re-discover hers after much personal tumult. According to Simon Barnes, "They both – separately? together? – felt the tug, the remembered love of the struggle, the sweet validation of victory, that glorious moment when you know that you are better than your opponent."

It was to be Clijsters who had the better of it on this day, a 2-6 6-2 6-3 success, in which she said she had initially been overwhelmed by the speed of Henin's game but that when she went for the lines with a bit more confidence and found them, the match turned in her favour. It did not help Henin's cause that she stumbled at one stage,

Justine Henin

Kim Clijsters

landing on her right elbow, a fall that was to have significant consequences.

No such interruptions for Serena Williams, though she had to withstand three set-points in the opening set to interrupt the increasingly confident flow of Maria Sharapova. This was a Sharapova still groping her way back after shoulder and elbow surgeries, who was not yet deemed a genuine contender but whose nostrils did flare that much wider when she returned to Centre Court, scene of her 2004 triumph, especially with Serena at the other end of the court, as it had been that day.

Yen-Hsun Lu

Chris McGrath, in *The Independent*, suggested that some of the rallies might have been directed by Alfred Hitchcock, so laden were they with heavy staccato exchanges. "It was a measure of the renewal in her game that Sharapova should claw her way back to three set points; and of its lingering frailties, that she ended up yielding Williams the chance she would take by again double-faulting."

Ostensibly, the difference was to be found in the weight and placement of the Williams serve. Had Serena's delivery ever been more consistent, more pronounced or carried more weight? What Caroline Wozniacki could have done with something like that in her armoury. The No.3 seed from Denmark was flattened by the Czech, Petra Kvitova, winning only two games. "Every shot, it was working" Kvitova said. Clearly.

Serena Williams

Maria Sharapova

Day **EIGHT**
29.06.2010

V. WILLIAMS
VS
PIRONKOVA

CLIJSTERS
VS
ZVONAREVA

KVITOVA
VS
KANEPI

S. WILLIAMS
VS
LI

Tsvetana Pironkova

Tuesday 29 June…

For Venus Williams and Kim Clijsters, this was the afternoon after the afternoon before. For Tsvetana Pironkova and Vera Zvonareva, nothing in tennis had tasted quite as sweet in their lives. The procession expected of the women's quarter-finals struck a couple of rocks in the road and two Grand Slam champions were unceremoniously tossed from the carriage.

Thinking of carriages, the second Tuesday always had something of an After The Lord Mayor's Show feel to it; nothing to do with the

participants, it was just that so much energy had been expended on the previous day, so much had happened that it was almost impossible to keep tabs on, there was bound to be something of a let down. A pair of the sports' finest were to feel that let down more than most.

Before all of that, though, there was time for more mature reflection on the previous day's events and how Andy Murray might fare now that he had reached the last eight of Wimbledon for the third successive time. A sense of balance was brought to the increasingly boisterous headlines by Jon

92

Henderson, one of the sport's finest writers, who had recently completed *The Last Champion, The Life of Fred Perry*, a brilliant book reflecting the life and times of Our Fred. Would it be Our Andy in 2010? Henderson provided a graphic background as to where we stood with the Murray phenomenon.

"There does seem, finally," Henderson wrote, "to be a general acceptance that the man and his tennis are both informed by a deep sense of doing things his way, which includes not always feeling the need to explain himself. Hence, we recently had the phoney drama of whether Murray was going to 'snub' the Queen on one of her rare visits to Wimbledon. In the event, not only did he bow but with a gratuitously theatrical flourish and then, after the match, chatted so easily and amicably with the monarch on the balcony of the All England Tennis Club, it would have been no surprise had a press release swiftly followed informing us that he and his girlfriend, Kim Sears, would be taking their post-Wimbledon holiday at Balmoral. And so it is that Murray's path to the heart of the British nation may not quite be sealed this year. But he is not far away."

Venus Williams

Of those left in the women's competition, who had the dearest place in this nation's affections? Well, the Williams sisters had been so dominant at The Championships in the past ten years, that they had won eight of the singles titles between them. There were those in the Venus camp, others liked Serena the better – she of the ridiculously square biceps. One wished one or the other the best but the secret hope was that they did not meet, for those matches had long since lost their original air of intrigue. In fact, they were now both shrill and dull.

Very few entering the grounds on this day, though, thought they would retire having seen a five time champion who had won 58 other career titles, receive such a whipping and from a player of whom so little was known – even in her native Bulgaria. Pironkova, a 23-year-old from Plovdiv, was ranked 80 spots below Venus and yet all the silverware in the world was no defence against someone palpably fitter, faster and sharper.

Venus did not quite know how to take defeat as much as she had been hazy in her pursuit of victory. She seemed, as Andy Bull in the *Guardian* reported, "To get caught up in her own confusion, unable to fathom just why her game was letting her down so. She struggled on her serve, as the sun faded in and out of the clouds, often blinding her as she tossed the ball up."

Yes, Pironkova had defeated Williams once before in a Grand Slam tournament, the first round of the 2005 Australian Open, but the seeds are often more vulnerable at that stage of a championship and especially in Melbourne which comes before anyone can find a degree of form. Though Williams said she could not remember that match – a case, quite probably of selective amnesia – Pironkova said that she recalled it brilliantly, and decided that her best means of victory was to move Venus around as much as possible, catch her off guard, keep her guessing.

While there was a sense that not all was well with the Williams physique – she often reached for the small of her back – she did not countenance an excuse for her lack lustre 6-2 6-3 defeat, a real smack across the cheek for someone of her pedigree. The tally of 29 unforced errors, though, made for depressing reading and the last of them was perhaps the worst, a curious dab of a forehand volley into the net on match point. Pironkova never looked as if she would let her off the hook and it still took nerve to approach for the kill.

Broken in the third game of the second set, the Bulgarian responded by salvaging a drop shot and when her lob landed just inside the baseline, the crowd's roar was like a shot of adrenalin to her. That set up the opportunity to retrieve the break and consecutive double faults from Venus in her next service game left her 2-4 down. It was an insurmountable challenge, despite Richard, her father, prompting "Come on V. Turn it up V."

"Why wouldn't I want to keep pursuing this?" Venus responded when questioned as to whether a defeat like this made her contemplate a wider picture. "Today, I didn't seem to be the best tennis player but for the most part I rock and roll this game."

➤

Vera Zvonareva

There was a last dance in this event, too, for Clijsters, who was once more left to consider that Wimbledon was the only one of the Grand Slams at which she had not been to the semi-finals. Zvonareva had been one of those players who ought to have done better in the majors, but had been hampered by a succession of injuries, especially to her wrist, that had seriously interrupted her career. Eager to make up for lost time, the Russian held her nerve after dropping the first set to emerge with a 3-6 6-4 6-2 success. "Are you as stunned as we are?" Clijsters, conceivably still a little rusty on the grass, was asked, first up. "Disappointed," was her response. "I wasn't able to come up with my best at the important times in the match".

And so the women's semi-finals would take on a very unlikely hue. Pironkova would play Zvonareva and Serena Williams would meet Petra Kvitova, of the Czech Republic, who emerged from the quarter-final that – at the outset of the championship – may have been beyond the powers of Paul The Octopus (about to replace Mystic Meg in the nation's soothsaying affections) to discern.

For anyone to suggest that Kvitova against Kaia Kanepi, of Estonia, represented their

Kim Clijsters

considered choice of a Wimbledon quarter-final, they would rightly have been led away probably mumbling something about Special K being their favourite breakfast cereal and that's when the idea struck them.

Kvitova had not won a match on grass before the week before The Championships and Kanepi had fought her way through qualifying and was thus bidding to become only the third woman in the Open Era to reach the last four of a Grand Slam having endured the pressures and perils of qualification. For the most part, too, it was Kanepi who seriously shaded what was a pretty scrappy affair.

She won the first set 6-4 after Kvitova had double-faulted at break point at 4-4, had match point three times in the second set tie-break, and sped to a 4-0 lead in the third set, too. Indeed, it was hard to believe a final 4-6 7-6 8-6 score line in the Czech's favour. In that final set, she was broken once, served for the set at 5-3, lost her nerve (and serve) once more, and spurned two further match points at 6-5. "I won without a serve," Kviktova said. Kanepi might have added that she would have won had she had one.

Away from all this fancy stuff, Serena Williams was getting on with her work in her own way, a simple 7-5 6-3 victory over Li Na, of China. There are certain things about the Williams' style which still made people's teeth grind, maybe it was the screaming, the muscle, the power, the brute force. Simplistically, a quarter of Serena's serves were unreturned by Li, she struck 11 aces and a single double fault. She was brilliant. ➢

Petra Kvitova

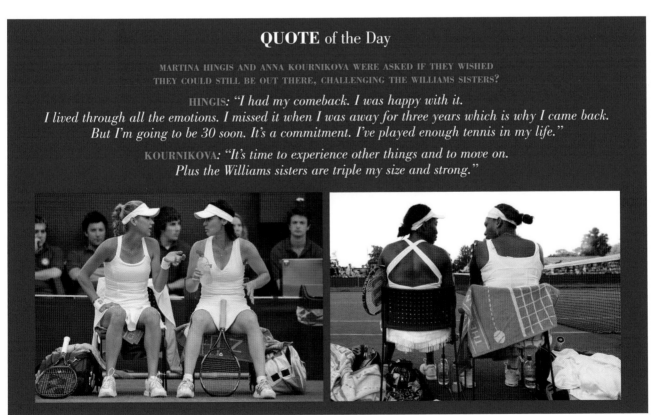

QUOTE of the Day

MARTINA HINGIS AND ANNA KOURNIKOVA WERE ASKED IF THEY WISHED THEY COULD STILL BE OUT THERE, CHALLENGING THE WILLIAMS SISTERS?

HINGIS: *"I had my comeback. I was happy with it. I lived through all the emotions. I missed it when I was away for three years which is why I came back. But I'm going to be 30 soon. It's a commitment. I've played enough tennis in my life."*

KOURNIKOVA: *"It's time to experience other things and to move on. Plus the Williams sisters are triple my size and strong."*

Serena Williams

If that was not enough, Martina Hingis and Anna Kournikova were back at SW19 and what a fuss they were causing. Veterans at the age of 29, the perennially youthful but long-retired Kournikova (her beau, Enrique Iglesias, was also in town) and Hingis, still constantly 're-emerging' after various career setbacks, were playing in the invitation doubles and whoever dreamed up that invitation was worth their weight in grounds passes.

Brendan Gallagher, of the *Telegraph*, was among many thirtysomethings enticed to Court No.2 "Hingis won the title here in 1997 and was seven times a Grand Slam champion although on the evidence of her recent performance on *Strictly Come Dancing*, not on the evidence of her dodgy footwork. Could the eyesight be going as well? One of her challenges was out by a yard, or perhaps she was gently showboating, something she never did as a stellar player. Kournikova plays her fair share of charity matches but amid the laughter and fun (against Britain's Anne Hobbs and Sam Smith) you could also sense a little yearning for what might have been. What this spice girl wants, what she really, really wants, is to be fit and injury free, like the golden teenager she once was."

Having run the rule over Hingis and Kornikova, the latter of whom still had trouble with 'five different things wrong with my back after two herniated discs' one was tempted to take a look over at junior competition and those, not a lot older than Hingis was when she lifted that first Grand Slam, as a 16-year-old in Australia in 1997, which she followed with success at Wimbledon and the US Open. Laura Robson, the 2008 junior girls' champion, was 16 now and thus people were taking here even more seriously than was the case two summers before.

Into the last 16 of this year's girls' event, Robson was one of five British youngsters, both male and female to reach this stage of the competition – more than any other country no less – which resonated nicely across in the LTA Members' enclosure on No.1 Court.

Robson was joined by Tara Moore and Eleanor Dean, the latter only 14 herself, who showed enormous poise to defeat Russia's Ksenia Kirillova 6-4 0-6 6-4. "Winning two rounds is unbelievable and whatever way it works out we can have a celebration at the end of the tournament," she said. In the boys' event, Oliver Golding and James Marsalek were doing their bit for the locals. "I think I can be a top 100 player now more than ever," Marsalek, 18, said.

It was a long way from the fourth round of the juniors to such a plateau but you had to admire young Marsalek's confidence. More of it, we cried.

Day **NINE**
30.06.2010

FEDERER
vs
BERDYCH

SODERLING
vs
NADAL

TSONGA
vs
MURRAY

DJOKOVIC
vs
LU

KUBLER
vs
GOLDING

Wednesday 30 June…

"I'm unhappy with the way I'm playing; I don't think I played poorly but I'm struggling with some injury issues which don't allow me to play the way I would like to play. Under the circumstances I think I played a decent match, you know. If I'm healthy I can handle them". Who said this at Wimbledon 2010? It sounded for all the world like one of the seven first round British casualties but no, this was a man chasing his seventh singles title, the imperious, but now seriously underwhelmed, Roger Federer.

Not since 2002, when he was beaten in the opening round by the 18-year-old Mario Ancic, of Croatia, had Federer failed to reach the last day of Wimbledon. Indeed the Swiss had won the title six years out of the last seven and despite considerable murmurings to the contrary – and the evidence of his shaky opening two rounds – most expected another final from him at the very least, now we were deep into The Championships. Then, along came Tomas Berdych.

According to Federer, along came a few back and leg issues, as well, which he had partly mentioned after his fourth round victory but then added quickly that he was over them. Obviously, as he struggled and stressed against the powerful flat hitter from the Czech Republic, the problems flared again. And it was too much for the champion to have to bear.

➢

Right: Tomas Berdych

Below: Roger Federer

Rafael Nadal

The historical connotations were all too evident. Nine years ago, that other Wimbledon legend, Pete Sampras, had lost a fifth set 7-5 on the same court against a young pretender called Federer to end a 31-match winning streak at Wimbledon having secured seven singles titles. He never won an eighth.

Though it took a huge leap of faith to suggest Berdych was going to set off on a succession of Wimbledon victories, here were echoes of that landmark event and just the hint of the end of an era, if not the passing of a baton. There were headlines suggesting that Roger had been a bad loser. . "The beginning of the end for the best ever player," *The Independent* intoned. The Crash of the Titan was the *Daily Mail*'s response; the tabloids loved 'Roger and Out' of course.

Indeed, over on No.1 Court at the time of the titan's crash, Patrick Kidd, of *The Times*, was following Rafael Nadal's intriguing progress against Robin Soderling, when a whisper of "Roger Out" circulated through the press seats. "It sounded like a party of airline pilots on a works outing," Kidd mused.

But this was no party, except if you happened to be tall, blond and from Valasske Mezirici in the Czech Republic. There were those who said they saw this coming. Nick Bollettieri, the master coach from the United States, was in full "I told you so" mode. To be fair, he had said on the eve of the tournament that if there was one player who could cause Federer problems it was Berdych (he did not mention Alejandro Falla or Ilija Bozoljac, but never mind).

Bollettieri then picked out seven elements that contributed to the Berdych victory, the most remarkable of which was that Federer ought to consider playing a double-handed backhand on the return of serve "two hands are better than one" the guru said. "Whoever you are – genius or no – you need not just to adapt but to realise you need to adapt. The power of the game these days has changed things."

This was incendiary indeed. Sampras never played with two hands, nor did McEnroe, nor Becker, nor Edberg but Bollettieri really believed that Federer should contemplate such a switch if he was to be able to hold off the aggressive, power hitters in the game today. One suspected that Roger would not be heading to Florida for a lesson any time soon.

There was not too much commiseration for Federer when he mentioned the extent to which he had been hampered by injuries, especially when on the face of it he had been outplayed and out-thought by Berdych. "Federer was hammered from pillar to post by a totally fearless and inspired opponent who respected the man across the net but not his reputation," Brendan Gallagher wrote in the *Telegraph*. "That takes bottle. Berdych marched onto Centre Court with a simple but effective plan – a big and clever server whose stinging weapon was a sledgehammer forehand whose main defence was a scrambling backhand and a heart the size of his native Prague."

Federer lost 6-4 3-6 6-1 6-4 and perhaps crucial to it was Berdych's response to an attack of the jitters at 2-3, love-40 down in the fourth set. A break there could have been the opportunity for a Swiss resurrection but, showing more of that subtlety, panache and courage, the Czech held strong.

While all this was going on, Nadal was having to extricate himself from his own spot of bother. There had been just 22 minutes of tennis on No.1 Court and Nadal was serving at 0-5, 30-40 against Soderling, with whom he was having a series of fascinating tussles. Then, the Swedish storm subsided while one from Spain began to take on an irresistible form.

A lesser mortal than Nadal might have given that first set away but he slowly maneuvered himself back into a succession of rallies and won three games in succession. He lost the set but he had a momentum. Soderling knew it, as did the crowd. That sense was emphasised in the first game of the second set when a ball which appeared long to the naked eye was not called. Nadal challenged and then freaked when Hawk-Eye showed that the ball had kissed the back extremity of the baseline. He felt the point should have been replayed but instead the umpire, believing that Nadal had completed his shot before the call came, gave Soderling a break point.

It was as if Nadal became Lou Ferrigno before one's very eyes. In a controlled Hulk-like rage, he won six points in succession and eventually completed a 3-6 6-3 7-6 6-1 victory. It remained, though, a curious match, packed with baseline hitting and yet devoid of unforgettable rallies, winners and unforced errors in equal supply. Nadal simply professed himself 'very happy' as was his wont.

For some reason, simple nerves surely, it was not a day when the best players in the world started well. Federer had lost the first set, so had Nadal and so did Andy Murray (Novak Djokovic was the notable exception, as he trounced Mr Lu, from Taiwan, in straight sets, of which a little more later).

There had been a considerable playing down in France of Jo-Wilfried Tsonga's hopes of delaying Murray's march into the semi-finals, too long; indeed one smelled a bit of a rat. *Rien de chance* our colleagues from France kept telling us that Tsonga had reached the finals of the Australian Open two years ago, the semi-finals this and did not seem to be unduly hampered by anything other than being the last player from his country in the event and thus encumbered by as much of the hope and expectation Murray suffered from.

The first set was a bit stifling. Tsonga had a set point at 5-4 which Murray saved with a forehand volley winner and followed up with a brace of aces. Into a tie-break we went in which the first four points were mini-breaks, Tsonga stealing a march when Murray netted a forehand before the first change of ends. It was an advantage the Frenchman was not to lose, settling the set when an excellent serve set up the chance for a backhand crosscourt volleyed winner.

Jo-Wilfried Tsonga

QUOTE of the Day

Q: (to JO-WILFRIED TSONGA) Everyone in Britain is getting excited about Murray winning Wimbledon. How do you rate his chances?

A: I hope it is gonna be him. I told him at the net. Make me a pleasure, go all the way. He's a good player and it's never easy to play in front of his crowd. He's really strong. I hope he will win."

Andy Murray

107

Novak Djokovic

As Simon Barnes wrote in *The Times*, "Tsonga carried away the first set with all-out blasting and a forehand that could go through the wall. The match turned on a single bizarre point in the second set tie-break. Murray, it has to be said, was playing some top quality stuff. Tsonga, continuing his policy of single-handedly reviving the serve and volley game had been picked off at the net a couple of times in the breaker. So in came the serve, the charge and then followed the great suicide leave, the shot that Tim Henman once made his own. An error forced by the gathering intensity of Murray's play. And after that Murray did what he can do better than anyone in the game: he simply dismantled the player opposite him."

The third game of the third set was the crux. Murray had five break points on which he either could not quite direct the ball as deep as he would have liked, or Tsonga took a risk and prospered. On the sixth, Tsonga was lured into a backhand volley he ought to have resisted and the Scot was ahead.

Then, horror of horrors, he attempted a drop shot on the first point of the next game and netted. In a flash, he was break points down, saving one with a backhand volley, and the second when the audacity of another drop shot was rewarded because, although Tsonga reached it, Murray had reacted perfectly to finesse a forehand volley into the open court. Once he had held then, there was only one winner.

Murray was to drop only three games from the last dozen in the match, saving the very best for last; a forehand from a yard beyond the baseline, delivered with both feet off the ground from a yard behind the baseline into the opposite forehand corner with more power generated than anything he had produced in the entire match.

The fourth quarter-final was to lack the sheer thrill of the first three, as Djokovic accounted for Yen-Hsun Lu, 6-3 6-2 6-2, a result that will not have thrilled Andy Roddick entirely. There may have been a gaggle of Taiwanese fans waving their country's flags and cooing encouragingly but they were little more than a colourful, novel backdrop to a performance from the Serbian that reeked of the self confidence he had spent such a long time groping for.

"It was so refreshing to perform in the way I did," Djokovic said. "For the past six months I've struggled with my performances but now I'm playing great. I would give everything to have the chance of playing in the Wimbledon final." He had put himself in with a very decent shout, certainly his best ever, as he prepared to face Berdych, the No.12 seed.

Not only did the No.1 seed in the men's singles bite the dust, the same was true of that in the boy's singles, too. There are high hopes in Australia for Jason Kubler, whose father passed away when the boy was eight years old and who has been raised by his Filipino mother into a very well-rounded and exceptional athlete. On this day, however, Britain's Oliver Golding, once a boy actor, was a touch too good, winning 4-6 6-3 7-5.

Yen-Hsun Lu

A pinch and a punch, the first of…well, you know the rest. *The Sun*, God Bless It, had a novel way with its banner headline. Hurray for Murray from Surrey, it ran, a tongue-in-cheek way of breathing fire and perhaps no little Scottish indignation into the following afternoon's semi-final between Britain's No.1 and the world No.1.

"Home Counties tennis maestro, Andy Murray, lifted England's sporting gloom last night as the Surrey-based Brit smashed his way into a mouth-watering last four showdown," etc. Well, I suppose the fact that he lived in Oxted gave the 'Home Counties' line some credence, but it was typically rapscallion, spirited stuff. One could not help but get into a bit of a frenzy about the impending last four match that – despite the valiant efforts of Serena Williams, Vera Zvonareva, Tsvetana Pironkova and Petra Kvitova on this second Thursday of The Championships – was almost all the media rage.

The columnists were examining every minute detail of what we could expect – mostly every minute detail of Andy Murray – and there were more words from those who didn't know anything about tennis than from the tennis correspondents themselves. Judy Murray was taking up as much newsprint as her famed son. In the *Daily Mail*, for instance, Jan Moir, one of their legion of fine writers, waxed especially lyrical. "Judy Murray nurtured, she did not crush or over-cultivate. In doing so, she helped her son become one of the best on the planet at what he does – he is the fourth-ranked tennis player in the world not fourth in the list to play Joseph in the school nativity play. And while they have had their problems, the robust Murrays seem well adjusted and happy. Well done, mum."

"I can't remember the last time I was in an argument with her," Andy was reported to have told his official biographer. "Genuinely can't remember. I never slammed a door. Never said 'I hate you'. I think my mum is the only person who gets me, who understands me really well."

There was a warning that it was best not to tune into the Murray-Nadal match on the radio while at the wheel, because listening to sport in that way affected drivers more than if they had touched a drop before they set out. The Transport Research Laboratory's Dr Nick Reed commented: ➤

QUOTE of the Day

JAMIE MURRAY, *Andy's brother, not looking forward to the big match on Friday. "The players' box is a tense place, believe me. You are riding with your emotions all the time, you know that any facial expression, any bit of behaviour that might be considered out of the ordinary can be captured on TV or by the photographers. Actually, I'd prefer to watch it on TV."*

Judy Murray and Kim Sears watch Andy in action, Jamie noticable by his absence!

Andy Murray warming up for
his game against Rafael Nadal

113

Tsvetana Pironkova

"At particularly tense times, like penalty shoot-outs or tie-breaks, it may be safer to find a safe place to park and enjoy the action without risking an accident."

The Mirror decided that every one of their readers ought to own a Murray mask and printed one, with the invaluable "How to Make it instructions" 1. Use scissors to cut along the dotted lines of Murray's face. Don't forget the eye-holes. 2. Trace around face on to a cardboard backing – perhaps an old cornflakes box – and then glue them together. 3. Pierce both sides of the mask and thread through enough elastic or rubber bands to ensure it fits snugly over your face. It was best to make the most of a free gift like this, because according to those who knew these things, on one legitimate sale-and-exchange site, tickets for Centre Court on Friday were priced at almost £4,000.

For those who had come out of the hat with the second Thursday, there was one name who was instantly recognisable and four who would probably pass along St Mary's Walk on most days without turning a head. First, Zvonareva would play Pironkova, the Bulgarian conqueror of Venus Williams who had to bring her head out of the clouds as quickly as she could. They would be followed onto court by Serena Williams, in her seventh Wimbledon semi-final against Kvitova, who had lost in her previous two appearances at the All England in the first round. No contest surely.

Well, in their rather different ways, they were both decent contests. For half an hour, Pironkova was so in the mood against Zvonareva that it looked as if she might give Serena the chance to avenge the stain on the family shield; or indeed for the world No.82 to stain it still further, by knocking out both the sisters.

➤

ROLEX

Serena Williams

Again showing scant respect for the rankings, Pironkova quickly began to stretch her more experienced opponent with some unerring baseline play and a very nice line in disguised drop shots. She won the first set 6-3. There was a sense that she had the Centre Court with her too, and it may have had something to do with the quiet calm of her game, one that did not need the recurring reinforcement of grunts, groans or shrieks.

Zvonareva was a little less muted thought it had to be said that the tennis the two produced was more of a throwback to less throaty times; the players were silky, slim, wore matching visors (a bit like Helen Wills Moody playing Helen Jacobs in the 1930s) and might have been contesting a club championship somewhere in the shires.

The excellence of their tennis was profound though, in Pironkova's case, it began to slide in the second set as Zvonareva began to find her range and won it with comparative ease and broke in the opening game of the third set by which time everyone had sensed that the result would be in her favour. It was – 3-6 6-3 6-2.

One had to admire the entrance that Kvitova made for her first appearance on the grandest of stages. She did not look perturbed to be playing the world No.1, indeed, the left-hander from the Czech Republic was all thrust and bustle. Kvitova, hoping to emulate Martina Navratilova who was also a) a leftie and b) from the Czech Republic, actually broke Williams to lead 3-2 in the first set. She was not afraid to show her feelings either, a nice fist pump greeting that breakthrough.

Kvitova simply had to win the first set to have a chance and even that may not have been enough protection. As it happened, Williams broke back in the eighth game with some meaty ground-strokes allied to a couple of tentative volleys from her opponent and the faint whiff of an upset was soon disappearing on the quickening Centre Court breeze.

After her 7-5 6-2 victory, it appeared that the greatest threat to a fourth title for Serena would be to expect it to happen, rather than make it so. "On paper, it looks as if I should win," she said of the final against Zvonareva. "The biggest thing is for me to stay positive and not put too much pressure on myself," Her opponent was warm in her congratulations. "Serena play very well today. Serena has many experiences. I think that Serena win here," Kvitova said before bidding her breakthrough Grand Slam farewell with a very healthy cheque for £250,000, more than half as much as she had earned in the sum total of her career before this fortnight.

At home, they will have been rejoicing in a player who would one day shine perhaps half as brightly as Navratilova once did. And how wonderful it was to see the nine-time singles champion on each and every day at Wimbledon, for Martina had learned six months earlier that ➤

Petra Kvitova

she had an early form of carcinoma, a breast cancer. "I got the good cancer," she said. "It turned out to be the best of the worst news. I'm done with everything, it's all behind me."

It was an opportunity to chat with her that could not be resisted – in fact it never could, not when she was growing up, when she played, when she won, when she lost (which did not happen that often as 167 singles titles testified). She reminded one of how her childhood was full of sponge baths and food queues, of how she took two trams and a train to get home from practice and the slog meant she treasured every moment spent on court. She said she could not believe that some coaches allowed youngsters to let the adults pick up balls during practice.

"Kids in the United States and Britain have it too easy," she said. "You are crazy in this country for tennis for two weeks and then you don't pay attention and this is why you don't have better players."

Well, there were the rumbles of something happening on the outside courts. It could have been the sound of potential salvation. The British were celebrating the first boy and girl to reach the semi-final in their events since Buster Mottram and Glynis Coles in 1972.

Oliver Golding was into the last four of the boys courtesy of a 4-6 6-4 6-4 victory over Renzo Olivo, a slight lad from Argentina. Laura Robson defeated Tara Moore, her fellow Brit, 7-5 6-1. The press was going gaga over Golding for the most part because he once co-starred with Christopher Lee in *The Adventures of Greyfriars Bobby* and had also appeared in the West End version of *Chitty Chitty Bang Bang*.

The 16-year-old certainly had a tendency to let things out; his temperament was noted at this year's Australian Open and is something he might work on improving. "I need to be comfortable in front of a crowd and acting has helped in that because I'm not daunted by it and can block it out," he said, "but I'm also less afraid to do things I shouldn't do, like getting angry during matches, showing my emotions too much and throwing my racket."

It was time to home for an early night to prepare for the men's semi-final on Friday that could change the way we saw tennis in Britain for a very long time. The debate on the airwaves was already underway. He could do it, couldn't he? Of course he could. No, it's Rafa he's playing, no chance. It made for a nervous night.

Martina Navratilova

Day **ELEVEN**
2.07.2010

DJOKOVIC
VS
BERDYCH

MURRAY
VS
NADAL

Andy Murray

The Times devoted a leader to the match. "Britain has not had a finalist since 1938, a statistic that haunts every British contender," **The Thunderer** said. "Beating Rafael Nadal – who is never outbattled and is a true champion in the wider sense – will require boldness as well as technical skill. If Andy Murray does ultimately triumph, perhaps the country will learn a lesson about how to win at sport: first understate, then overachieve."

The sense of anticipation was raw. The end of the afternoon was rawer still. Unfortunately, Murray could not overachieve. Rafael Nadal was not going to allow the fevered strains of British desire to sweep him out of the tournament any more than he was intent on bowing to Murray's class or fortitude.

Those of us who had looked at the basic tennis facts, who had ridden so many journeys with these two players over the past eight years, who had an idea of what the game was about, were never quite as confident about a Murray victory as some of those who visited tennis when there was nothing else to cover. I ventured that our boy would win a set, but to beat Nadal, this Nadal, in this mood, on this court, at this time, would have required a monumental performance of which even he did not seem yet equipped to produce. I would gladly have been wrong.

We could all be wise after the event, of course. It was just that having been in close proximity to the Nadal camp, spoken to the man himself, chatted to Toni, his uncle and coach, for quite a while and felt the good vibes from them all, there was an enveloping sense of destiny about the group. They believed; Britain hoped.

Nadal had remarked that the Centre Court was perfect 'there is a bit of clay behind the lines, no?' he said, smiling and the crust that had formed on the baseline as a result of so many hours of uninterrupted sunshine had provided as secure a foothold as any player could wish for. Remarkably, there were more complaints about the slippery nature of the clay of Roland Garros this year than there had been about the grass of SW19.

Nadal against Murray was the second semi-final and, as was their wont, the scheduling committee chose to save the better match for last, which was no disrespect to either Novak Djokovic or Tomas Berdych, it was just the way it was. The BBC wanted its tea-time audience to put the kettle on, settle back, relax (hopefully) and enjoy. They probably would have wished that Djokovic and Berdych would have kept on playing a little longer, but this was to be another day of simplified semis.

Remarkably, Murray's four-set delay of Andy Roddick's progress to the final in 2009 had been a bit of a novelty. Other than that, there had only been two men's semis that lasted more than three sets in eight years. In 2005, when Roddick ➤

defeated Thomas Johansson, of Sweden, and, three years earlier – Xavier Malisse, of Belgium, losing in five to Argentina's David Nalbandian.

We shall return to the first semi-final a little later. For it was the second that captivated the nation for two hours and 21 minutes until we had to tick off another year when our very Wimbledon best came up a fraction short. Nadal won the match 6-4 7-6 6-4; each set was tight, one or two shots here and there were the difference and, unfortunately, it was the Spaniard who tended to make them.

As the two men embraced at the net and Nadal expressed sorrow for what he had done, any sadness for Murray was tempered by the fact that the player had not been born who could deal with Nadal in this kind of mood. Murray's tendency, his style, his basic instinct, was to hold back and it was extremely hard, at any stage of one's life – certainly on Centre Court in a Wimbledon semi-final – to do something that ran counter to what came naturally.

Of the myriad half chances he had to spike Nadal's guns, many were lost because Murray could not quite bring himself to go for the jugular. He had take on the occasional forehand, indeed he started in particularly rapacious style, but at the crunch times, when he should have rammed home his advantage in a rally, he opted for safety.

"When Rafael Nadal waters his plants, he probably uses a water cannon," Oliver Holt wrote in *The Mirror*. "When he eats a 16-ounce steak, he probably swallows it whole. The bloke Andy Murray played yesterday was no ordinary tennis player. It was Conan The Tennis Player. It was a man whose displays of raw power made the genteel crowd titter nervously in their seats."

And yet, for periods, Murray was there with him, stride for muscly stride, hitting just as effectively.

The first two sets were critical, of course, for to fall two sets adrift of Nadal surely meant that the match would be beyond him. Having served out to love in the seventh game, there were half chances in the eighth, an unforced forehand error at 30-all, a backhand service return on a second serve at 40-30, all of these could have changed the complexion in Murray's favour in the opening set; instead it was Nadal who struck first.

Murray should not have been broken, not with two aces in the game, but he double faulted his advantage away and the Spaniard pounced, a forehand service return so deep it provided the opening for a forehand winner and, on the first break point of the match, Murray erred on his forehand flank. Nadal required three set points to clinch the set, doing so when a ding-dong rally ended with another Murray forehand mistake.

In the second set, too, Murray's serve started brilliantly, he held his first three service games to love. At deuce on the Nadal serve, at 3-3, the big man slipped but still reached a drop shot only for Murray's resultant lob to land just long. He held on despite not making a first serve on the last four points. Murray held to 15, without making a single first serve. He was desperate for a chance. Along came a couple of them.

At 15-40, tension mounted. A mobile phone trilled on the first break chance and Murray's forehand service return thudded into the net; on the second, Nadal used his own forehand to move Murray around to the extent that he miscued on a backhand. He had seen off the danger momentarily and the set entered a tie-break. This had to be all or nothing.

Murray led 2-0 but the forehand let him down again and it was 2-2. Nadal led 4-3 but two Murray aces meant it was back to 5-4 in his favour. He tried a drop shot, Nadal reached it, quite incredibly, but the Spaniard double-faulted to give Murray a set point. He missed his first serve just when he wanted one and, after a forehand from Nadal into Murray's forehand corner prompted a clipped response, Nadal was there with a backhand volley, no less, to cut off the chance. A backhand pass from Nadal caught the tape, set point to him. Nadal's forehand into the Murray backhand corner bounced twice before the scurrying Scot could reach it. Nadal led by two sets to love.

Boris Becker, three times the champion, stressed what could have made a difference on that Murray point. "If he had put a big serve in the corner, only for Nadal to rip a return past him, he would have to hold his hands up and say 'too good,'" the German reflected. "But he missed his first serve, played a tentative second and retreated three yards behind the baseline. Just then, he let Nadal do the talking and he was always going to lose that point."

Understandably a little relaxed, Nadal promptly lost his first service game in the third set to love ➤

David Beckham with his son, Brooklyn

and Murray was once more holding serve almost for fun until the eighth game and the moment the match was ended. A forehand winner from Nadal set up a break point saved by a 118 mph serve down the T. But Murray double-faulted to give his opponent a second break chance and this time the home man netted a forehand from a backhand slice that landed like a feather on his side of the net.

Nadal was the win the last four games of the match, the clinching forehand error from Murray causing him to respond in much the manner as he had when defeating Roger Federer in the final two summers earlier. Britain's dream had been crushed once more.

We tried our best at gallows humour. In a cartoon in the *Telegraph* the brilliant Matt pictured an umpire announcing "Based on the second preference system, Murray is the winner." The blame game led to David Beckham, who had been part of the England coaching set up at the World Cup (and look how that ended) being made the scapegoat for coming to the match to show solidarity with Murray.

Novak Djokovic

Ostensibly, Murray was beaten by a better player and in that there was no shame, if a few regrets. "I obviously want to win for myself, I want to win for the guys I work with, I want to win for the UK," he said. "It's a little more disappointing to lose here than the other slams because this is the biggest one of the year for me. It's tough. I'll work hard and hope that it doesn't happen again."

In the final, Nadal would play Berdych, the Czech, who had shown that his defeat of Federer in the quarter-finals was no flash-in-the-pan as he squeezed the life out of Djokovic, 6-3 7-6 6-3. Signs of the nervy Berdych we had anticipated were dismissed in a solid, uncomplicated first service game followed by one from Djokovic that was terribly erratic, a double fault, an ace, a couple of wobbly, reckless forehands.

Throughout, Berdych played splendidly, although it had to be said that the Serb tended to make his life a little easier by offering up a performance that emphasised the doubts that continued to swirl around in his head. How about the wildly missed overhead to save a second break point when the second set tie-break was tied at 5-5? That is what the big occasion could do, even to a world No.3, who had beaten his opponent twice previously in straight sets.

In that tie-break, Berdych held and lost four consecutive set points – two on his own serve with his right arm suddenly becoming all jelly-like – in what became one of the classic showdowns of The Championships. On the fourth point, there was a huge rally, the last shot of which, a defensive Djokovic lob, landed smack on the baseline, only for it to be called out. Djokovic challenged, successfully, but was informed he had to replay the point. Oh, the unfairness of it all.

Djokovic had a set point of his own, wiped out by a forehand volley winner from Berdych, proving his all-court qualities. Next a fifth set point to Berdych but he netted a backhand, even though there was a gap. A second to Djokovic, but a ferocious off-forehand brought a backhand error. Finally a sixth opportunity fell to Berdych at which Djokovic double-faulted. We had seen it all, and more.

Day **TWELVE**
3.07.2010

S. WILLIAMS
VS
ZVONAREVA

LINDSTEDT AND TECAU
VS
MELZER AND
PETZSCHNER

KING AND SHVEDOVA
VS
VESNINA AND
ZVONAREVA

BURTON AND MORGAN
VS
HELLER AND KRAWIETZ

BROADY AND
FARQUHARSON
VS
BIRYUKOV AND
RUMYANTSEV

The Royal Box was choc-a-bloc with former lady champions, the foremost of whom was the Chairman's Special Invitee, Evonne Goolagong-Cawley, the third of eight children from an Australia-Aboriginal family, who once peered through the fence at a local tennis court in Barellan, New South Wales and was invited by a kindly local resident to come and play. It had been three decades since Mrs Cawley became only the second mother to win the title and she had her 29-year-old son, Morgan, with her to enjoy the festivities.

Being an outsider looking in was something that Serena Williams could easily relate to. The story of the Williams sisters and their development on rock-hard, run down, dismal courts in Compton, California was as much a part of tennis folklore as that of the wonderful Evonne, who now had a tennis park named after her at home.

There were courts across the world these days named after Suzanne Lenglen, Rod Laver, Margaret Court, Arthur Ashe and Philippe Chatrier. Surely one would have to be found on which either Venus or Serena, perhaps both, could have their names placed up in lights. That was the way they liked it, after all.

But Centre Court remained Centre, with no adornments necessary. It had long become the sisters' favourite place to play, where their innate sense of belonging found its true reflection, where they relished the hold they had had over the sport for more than a decade. Where, indeed, they liked to show off.

The 2010 final would pit Serena against Vera Zvonareva, the Russian, who had twice been to the fourth round of The Championships, but in eight years on the Sony Ericsson WTA Tour, had made just a single Grand Slam semi-final, at the 2009 Australian Open, where she was denied the chance of meeting Serena in the final by Dinara Safina, her compatriot (and what in the Lord's name had happened to her?).

The chances were always that it might not be a final which would evoke many lasting memories for Serena; finals against anyone these days tended to be short-lived and rather punishing experiences. Brutality is not as word that sat easily with a feminine sport, but there were few more apt ways of describing the force of the onslaught waged by Serena and with which she reclaimed the Wimbledon title writing her name ever more boldly into the history books.

Long had been the assertion that the sisters had not simply raised the bar when it came to power and physicality in the women's game; instead with the most forceful and full blown forehands, they had smashed it high into the air and never again would it likely return to its former level.

For 67 minutes on a sunny summer's afternoon (weren't they all?) Serena battered and pushed the unfortunate Zvonareva into submission with a relentless barrage that brought the younger sister her fourth Wimbledon singles title and 13th major crown. Nick Pitt, in the *Sunday Times*, wrote, "There was not much art, not much music except for the percussion of the heavy guns. So can anyone grasp the nettle and rid us of further non-contests and bring back the beautiful game? A glance up at the Royal Box where a clutch of former champions sat encouraged the belief that a really gifted player could spike the Williams guns. Martina Navratilova would attack the net and Billie Jean King would surely have found a way to turn the Williams power against its originator."

Nine aces from Serena took her total for the tournament to a Wimbledon record of 89 and it was that serve that kept Zvonareva pinned on the back foot, unable to get in the first strike that might have allowed her to gain some confidence. When Williams broke in the eighth game with an unstoppable forehand pass, the result became some of a formality. Though Zvonareva saved two set points at 5-3 down, a smash and another belter of a forehand winner sealed the set, which Williams built upon with an immediate break in the second.

Knowing that staying focused on the point in hand rather than thinking too far ahead and forming a premature image of victory was almost as dangerous as the opposition, Williams did not take a step back. And soon, Zvonareva became almost submissive in the way she approached the points, pushed deeper and deeper into a defensive mode from which it would become impossible to break.

Two thudding overheads from the champion ended it all, flying past the outstretched Russian's, racket and crunching into the backstop. It was all over a shade too quickly and Williams was into her usual, a touch awkward, pirouette while Zvonareva, characteristically, sat with head in towel, letting her emotions flow. It had been a painful experience.

A first service percentage of 86 for Serena was phenomenal and when she landed that serve, only on two did she fail to win the point. There were 29 outright winners to nine from Zvonareva, and she won the point on all 14 of her net approaches. Clearly, this had been a lesson in sustained quality.

Even her father, Richard, did not quite know how long she could continue to play this well. "What is really amazing to me is that when an athlete gets to the levels that Venus and Serena have reached, the tendency is for them not to be as hungry as before but they don't show that at all. They just love to win." Richard knew from the moment she re-entered the gates three weeks before that his younger daughter would take an awful lot of shifting. "Serena wanted to win so badly and when it was time for practice she would say 'I don't want anyone talking. I want everyone quiet. I can win this tournament'. I could say things, like 'look at the ball,' but that was really it. Only myself, her mum and her trainer could come onto her court." ➤

Serena Williams

Vera Zvonareva

Remarkably, Richard expressed surprise that his daughters entered The Championships as the top two seeds for the first time since 2002. "Very much so, because most athletes can't maintain that kind of stamina either in their minds or their brains and with the problems they had, with Serena's knee hurting and Venus' hip hurting, it is truly wonderful they have done this," he said. "Every year they come back is a major surprise for me. I'm old now (nearly 70). I wonder how long I can do this."

One could not imagine the sisters ever trusting themselves to anyone other than Richard or his former wife, Oracene, who always travel with them to the Australian and French Opens. As for Serena, what could she tell of her continued sense of motivation? "It sounds ridiculous but I mostly do this because I want to look good," she said "When I am running around I am not thinking about winning Wimbledon, I am thinking about looking good when I am wearing my bikini. It keeps me extremely motivated.

"I want to live a fit life and it helps keep the injuries away. Staying fit and being healthy just makes life a lot easier. I can almost fit into a sample size when I need to borrow clothes from different designers. It is just better for my lifestyle. This is the most consistently fit I have been, so that is really important."

There were two other finals to play on Centre Court, as well as a host of goings-on on the outside courts. The men's doubles final pitted two people who had played singles on the Centre already in the tournament, Jurgen Melzer (who lost to Roger Federer) and Philipp Petzschner (beaten by Rafael Nadal) against two who were completely foreign to the surroundings, Robert Lindstedt, of Sweden, and Romania's Horia Tecau (though the latter was twice a former Wimbledon Boys' Doubles champion).

As we had been told time and again by the British authorities that doubles was almost as important as singles – especially with the money being pumped into it – it was somewhat ironic that the Wimbledon final should involve four such disparate figures. This was the first season together for Melzer and Petzschner, though they had won a title already, in Zagreb. ➤

Above: Winner of The Rolex Wimbledon Picture of the Year Competition 2010

Photographer: Hiromasa MANO (mannys@attglobal.net)

Jurgen Melzer and Philipp Petzschner

Vania King and Yaroslava Shvedova

This was the third successive men's final where at least one of the competitors had a 'z' in their surname (Nenad Zimonjic of Serbia played in 2008 and '09) and though there had been other such finalists (Raul Ramirez, Pancho Gonzalez and Balazs Taroczy), the Wimbledon compendium informed me that there had never been a case where both winners' surnames contained the last letter of the alphabet. History had been made.

Melzer – the Boys Singles champion here in 1999 – and Petzschner won 6-1 7-5 7-5. The victory was more one-sided than it read for their left-right partnership was cutting enough to have evoked memories of McEnroe and Fleming and Woodbridge and Woodforde. They were fast, hard-hitting and utterly confident. "We played incredible tennis," Petzschner said, "we may do this again."

The rapid Lindstedt-Tecau demise was rather a pity for they had been outstanding on their run to the final, not least when they came back from two sets and a match point down to defeat Max Mirnyi and Mahesh Bhupathi in the round of 16.

There were new champions in the Ladies Doubles as well (and another Z in the final). A dismal day for Vera Zvonareva was completed when she and fellow Russian, Elena Vesnina, were beaten 7-6 6-2 by Vania King, of the USA, and Yaroslava Shvedova, of Kazhakstan, who had teamed up together on a whim in Birmingham two weeks earlier, reached the semi-finals there and gone one better, getting to the final in s'Hertogenbosch, in the Netherlands, the weekend before Wimbledon. Only natural, then, they should win this week.

They were asked if they had ever set one or both feet on Centre Court? "No, I never even saw it before," said Miss King, by which you presumed she meant from the inside. "I only saw it from the players' restaurant," Miss Shvedova added. How did it feel to be a Wimbledon champion? "Kind of scary," Miss King said. "But this is what we work for. I love play with Slava. We are great friends."

A late evening stroll through the grounds brought one to Court No.5, and a boisterous crowd very much into what they were watching. Sadly, one had missed the progress of Lewis Burton and George Morgan, of Britain, into the Boys' Doubles final. And how creditably they had performed, surviving a gruelling three sets against Peter Heller and Kevin Krawietz, the No.5 seeds, from Germany, winning 15-13 in the third. Here, in their footprints were Liam Broady and Tom Farquharson, another British pair, facing the Russians, Mikhail Biryukov and Alexander Rumyantsev, and they led by a set and 4-1. It was time for an ice cream and a few moments of relaxation.

Just then, the Russian bears began to stir, enough to win the second set tie-break and threaten a nice British story. But Broady and Farquharson showed they were made of stern stuff, recovering to win 6-0 6-7 6-4. So we would have a British winner for certain, two of them in fact. Heady days.

FINAL Day
4.07.2010

BERDYCH
VS
NADAL

Rafael Nadal was apologetic. We sat together in a room off the players' lawn three days before the start of The Championships and he kept being distracted by the TV in the corner showing Germany against Serbia in the World Cup. The recording was one you did not want to wipe off, with its constant interruptions of "Woooahhh" and "Yeeeeh" as the football action unfolded. But Nadal did not want us to think he was taking the interview lightly and passed on a message to that effect.

It was no bother, actually. The world No.1 had even paused later to allow our photographer to spray his face and hair with water so that the pictures to accompany the article would have a more dramatic effect. It was a sign, surely, that the 24-year-old Spaniard was at peace with his surroundings, with himself and with his return to the scene of his most perfect tennis triumph, in 2008.

Sixteen days on and Nadal was restored to Centre Court for the fourth consecutive final in a championships at which he had competed. When you thought about it, it was an astonishing achievement in itself. No Spaniard had been this consistent at Wimbledon – the nearest being Conchita Martinez reaching the 1993 women's semi-final before winning the crown a year later.

His opponent would be Tomas Berdych, the No.12 seed from the Czech Republic, who came into his first such Grand Slam occasion on the back of beating two players from the top four, Roger Federer (who would be relegated to No.3 in the world when the new rankings were announced on the day after Wimbledon) and Novak Djokovic (about to be promoted to No.2). Asked for his opinion, the steadfast No.4 Andy Murray simply said, "I love the guy (Nadal). As a player, Rafa is the best thing that has ever happened to tennis. I play so much of the sport but he is the only guy I love to watch. Of course, I hate losing but when the match is finished I have so much respect for him."

There was no doubting that, in tennis, respect for Nadal had grown immeasurably. In the exasperating 11 months from May 2009 to April 2010, he had not won a title but felt he was giving himself a chance by reaching the semi-finals of several events, so he was a contender. Then came Monte Carlo, Rome, Madrid and Paris – four events, four clay court titles and only two sets dropped. He was right back in the mix.

That the final was to be something of an anti-climactic end to such an extraordinary few days was neither his fault, nor that of Berdych. It is simply that we were raising it to a pre-conceived level to which it would struggle to attain. Berdych needed to win the first set; he could not. He had to win the second; he did not. He had to ruffle Rafa in the third. It was beyond him. ➤

..., Nadal's 6-3 4-9(?) 6-4 victory was light years poorer than the Spaniard's 2008 classic with Federer. Not once in the entire enterprise did either man choose to serve and volley, the first time that had happened in a Wimbledon men's final since Lleyton Hewitt dismantled David Nalbandian from the baseline in 2002. It was, you might suppose, a recognition of the culture of caution that had gripped a game where once daring was rewarded with not only victory, but the appreciation of the sport's loyal following. The crowd desperately wanted varied entertainment, and a fight. They did not get much of either.

Nadal deserved Wimbledon's first £1 million winner's cheque, of course – a smattering of his winners were as good as any he had hit in the fortnight – but the heavier balls and slower surfaces were partly to blame for some of the sterility of the modern grass-court game. The advances in technology, too, played a part.

There were flashes of brilliance, including a stunning cross-court winner by the Spaniard to finish the job – and a forward roll (did it not remind you of your introduction to PE at primary school?) towards his family and backroom team to celebrate the culmination of two roller coaster weeks in which he twice flirted with a premature exit before finding his championship game.

For Berdych, with glory to be had, he took few risks on an afternoon of intermittent gusts of wind,

and paid for his caution. He won the first service game of the final to love, as false a dawn as the tournament has offered. There was an average of an ace a game from Nadal in the first set but he was also picking up points on 87 second deliveries, which suggested his opponent was more than a touch nervous.

In the seventh game, Berdych played his first really poor shot of the match – a backhand that landed five yards long – and was quickly 40-0 down on his own serve. On the second break point, Nadal's superb backhand return forced the blond giant into a forehand error. On a second set point two games later, it was once again the quality of the Nadal return that lulled his opponent into error.

If the challenger was to have an opportunity, he had to have taken one of three opportunities at the start of the second set. Nadal may have been a set up but he was not settled, his shots were landing half way up the court, he knew that if he gave Berdych an incentive, he might just take it. He started to play conservatively. But Berdych either could not, or would not, snap out of his own torpor.

Nadal handed the break points out, Berdych lobbed them straight back at him. The chance to seize the initiative resisted, Nadal kept his nose in front and extended it further towards the finish line when he broke to love and clinched the set in the 12th game, by far Berdych's worst of his last three

Thomas Berdych

matches. With that, of course, Nadal had the advantage of serving first in the third set as well – and was threatened only once, slicing so low on a break point in the third game that Berdych could only summon a weak, netted backhand in response. Yes, the Czech plugged down the occasional ace to keep himself honest, but as the set neared its end there was a perceptible rise in Nadal's ground-stroke grunting. He knew he was close. Berdych did too and once he had thrashed a forehand long to give Nadal his first match point, it was duly seized on by a whipping forehand crosscourt winner, the kind that only he can play.

Some champion, some man. The loser, who had looked resigned to his fate long before the finish, would at least know he could reach this level after so many disappointments. He knew what he could do in the future. The winner needed no such assurance. Nadal did enough to get the job done and could go into the second half of the summer comfortable in the knowledge that there did not appear to be many out there who could test him when it mattered. The US Open was up next, and also his attempt to become the seventh player in history to complete the box-set of Grand Slam tournaments.

"I am going to learn many things" Berdych said.

"It is about the experience of stepping onto a court like this and playing my first final of a Grand Slam. I have to get myself into a position to play more of these matches." He would loved to have joined Jan Kodes, his compatriot, who was watching from the Royal Box, as one of only seven men to win Wimbledon without playing a grass court match after the French Open. He may have decided to prepare differently next year, who knows?

Nadal had seemed hesistant at the outset and at various times during the match he did not place his finest foot forward. "If you are not nervous in a Wimbledon final, I think you are not human," he said. "I was a little bit lucky in a few moments but I have just tried my best in practice, in the matches, all the time. Every one of these is more special and this was not an easy year for me. To finish with the trophy here is really amazing. I didn't expect anything before the match, except to fight on every point like it was the last.

"If you want to play well, you have to find a way to win. I move very well on this court and that is very important for me. It is important to play on grass a little bit more aggressively than on the other surfaces. But the main thing is to want to improve all the time. Now it is time to enjoy the beach, fishing, golf, friends, party and Majorca." ➤

Leander Paes and Cara Black

Timea Babos and Sloane Stephens

Yevgeny Kafelnikov and Wayne Ferreira

Marton Fucsovics

For others, their moments of glory on the last day of The Championships were still to come. The mixed doubles final was won by Leander Paes, of India, and Cara Black, of Zimbabwe, two perennial Grand Slam favourites. Paes was the Wimbledon Boys' winner in 2000 and had spent most of the intervening years accruing his fortune from doubles, as had Black, of the famed tennis-playing family. They defeated Wesley Moodie, of South Africa, and Lisa Raymond, of the USA, 6-4 7-6.

Hungary had its first Boys' Champion when Marton Fucsovics, the No.13 seed, defeated Benjamin Mitchell, the unseeded Australian, 6-4 6-4. "I hope I can be the first very good player from my country," he said. Balazs Taroczy may have enjoyed that one. Though Mitchell lost, it was an encouraging day for the 1987 Men's champion, for he was a product of the Pat Cash International Academy on the aptly-named Hope Island, in Queensland.

"The most important thing is that Ben appreciates this is a great experience," Cash, who won this title himself 28 years before, said. "The tough job will come with the transition to the main ATP Tour which requires work, commitment and a fierce determination. Good on you Ben. The Aussies are on their way back."

If that was so, what about the Brits? Liam Broady and Tom Farquharson's 7-6 6-4 victory in the all-

British final against Lewis Burton and George Morgan was enough to merit a standing ovation on No.1 Court and front page news in the following morning's *Daily Mail*. Acclaim did not come much grander than that.

These left-handed girls from the Czech Republic were all the rage. Notwithstanding Petra Kvitova's success in reaching her first Grand Slam semi-final in the Women's Singles, Kristyna Pliskova, a semi-finalist at this year's Australian junior championships, edged out Sachie Ishizu of Japan, 6-3 4-6 6-4 to win the Girls' Singles crown. There was further success for Hungary in the Girls' Doubles as Timea Babos and American partner, Sloane Stephens, defeated Irina Khromacheva, of Russia, and Elina Svitolina, of Ukraine, the top seeds.

If Wimbledon was a showcase for all that was rich and rare in the juniors, it offered those grand old favourites from the game a chance to roll back the years. It was especially pleasing to see the former world No.1, Yevgeny Kafelnikov, of Russia, back on stage after a few years devoted to poker, though he and Wayne Ferreira, of South Africa, were pipped at the post in the Gentleman's Invitation Doubles by the American pair, Don Johnson and Jared Palmer, 6-3 6-2.

And was there a greater pick-me-up than the victory for Martina Navratilova and Jana Novotna in the Ladies' Invitation Doubles? What memories these two evoked and it was no slight on the pair

Jana Novotna and Martina Navratilova

Stefan Olsson and Robin Ammerlaan

Liam Broady and Tom Farquharson

Sharon Walraven and Esther Vergeer

Mark Woodforde and Pat Cash

they defeated in the final, Tracy Austin and Kathy Rinaldi-Stunkel that the 7-5 6-0 victory for Navratilova/Novotna was cheered to the echo.

There was a distinct freshness about the Gentlemen's Senior Invitation Doubles that we had not seen for a while and what a victorious team it produced, as Australia's Pat Cash and Mark Woodforde, they of innumerable Grand Slam titles, defeated Britain's Jeremy Bates and his Swedish partner, Anders Jarryd, 6-2 7-6.

The Dutch were to receive a bad press a week after Wimbledon for their football team's performance in the World Cup final, but in wheelchair tennis, the country had no peer. There were four 'finals' in the event, two in the men's, which were won by Robin Ammerlaan (Netherlands) and Stefan Olsson (Sweden) over Japan's Shingo Kunieda and Stephane Houdet, of France, (6-4 7-6) and by Maikel Scheffers and Ronald Vink (Netherlands) against the French pair, Frederic Cattaneo and Nicolas Peifer (6-1 6-4).

In the Ladies, the irrepressible Esther Vergeer and Sharon Walraven (Netherlands) beat Britain's Lucy Shuker and Daniela De Toro, of Australia, 6-2 6-3 while, in the other half of the draw, Aniek Van Koot, of Netherlands, and Annick Sevenans, of Belgium, were 6-3 6-7 6-4 victors over Jiske Griffioen (The Netherlands again) and Florence Alix-Gravellier, from France.

FASCINATING REVELATION of the Day

JOHN ISNER *(remember him?) had been making the most of his 15 minutes – or should that be 11 hours? – of fame. He had been doing the celebrity circuit back in the United States, throwing the first pitch for the New York Yankees baseball team at Yankee Stadium, appearing on the chat show circuit and dating actress, Kristen Stewart, from the Twilight move, Eclipse "She's really cool and all my friends are very jealous," he said.*

NICHOLAS MAHUT *of France had spent a few days in Boulogne, licking his wounds. A French writer said: "He was famous for a night, but the public weren't bothered. He lost, didn't he?"*

143

Rafael Nadal
The Gentlemen's Singles

Serena Williams
The Ladies' Singles

Philipp Petzschner & Jurgen Melzer
The Gentlemen's Doubles

Yaroslava Shvedova & Vania King
The Ladies' Doubles

Leander Paes & Cara Black
The Mixed Doubles

Jared Palmer & Donald Johnson
The Gentlemen's Invitation Doubles

Sloane Stephens & Timea Babos

The Girls' Doubles

Liam Broady & Tom Farquharson

The Boys' Doubles

Pat Cash & Mark Woodforde

The Gentlemen's Senior Invitation Doubles

Jana Novotna & Martina Navratilova

The Ladies' Invitation Doubles

Kristyna Pliskova

The Girls' Singles

Marton Fucsovics

The Boys' Singles

Esther Vergeer & Sharon Walraven

The Wheelchair Ladies' Invitation Doubles

Stefan Olsson & Robin Ammerlaan

The Wheelchair Gentlemen's Invitation Doubles

CHAMPIONSHIP RECORDS 2010

EVENT I – THE GENTLEMEN'S SINGLES CHAMPIONSHIP 2010
HOLDER: ROGER FEDERER

The Winner became the holder, for the year only, of the CHALLENGE CUP presented by The All England Lawn Tennis and Croquet Club in 1887. The Winner received a silver replica of the Challenge Cup. A Silver Salver was presented to the Runner-up and a Bronze Medal to each defeated Semi-finalist. The matches were the best of five sets.

First Round	Second Round	Third Round	Fourth Round	Quarter-Finals	Semi-Finals	Final

EVENT II – THE GENTLEMEN'S DOUBLES CHAMPIONSHIP 2010
HOLDERS: DANIEL NESTOR & NENAD ZIMONJIC

The Winners became the holders, for the year only, of the CHALLENGE CUPS presented by the OXFORD UNIVERSITY LAWN TENNIS CLUB in 1884 and the late SIR HERBERT WILBERFORCE in 1937. The Winners received a silver replica of the Challenge Cup. A Silver Salver was presented to each of the Runners-up, and a Bronze Medal to each defeated Semi-finalist. The matches were the best of five sets.

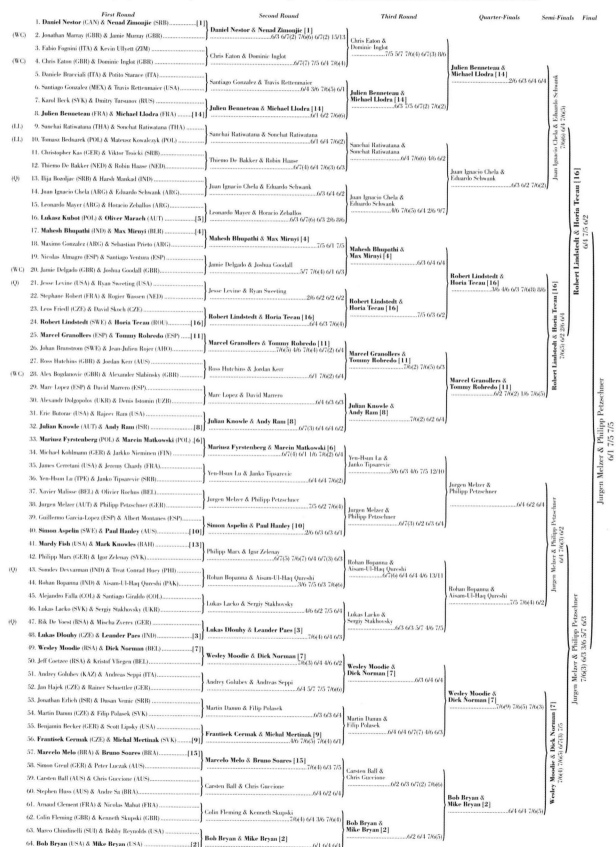

Heavy type denotes seeded players. The figure in brackets against names denotes the order in which they have been seeded. (WC)=Wild card. (Q)=Qualifier. (LL)=Lucky loser.

EVENT III – THE LADIES' SINGLES CHAMPIONSHIP 2010
HOLDER: SERENA WILLIAMS

The Winner became the holder, for the year only, of the CHALLENGE TROPHY presented by The All England Lawn Tennis and Croquet Club in 1886. The Winner received a silver replica of the Trophy. A Silver Salver was presented to the Runner-up and a Bronze Medal to each defeated Semi-finalist. The matches were the best of three sets.

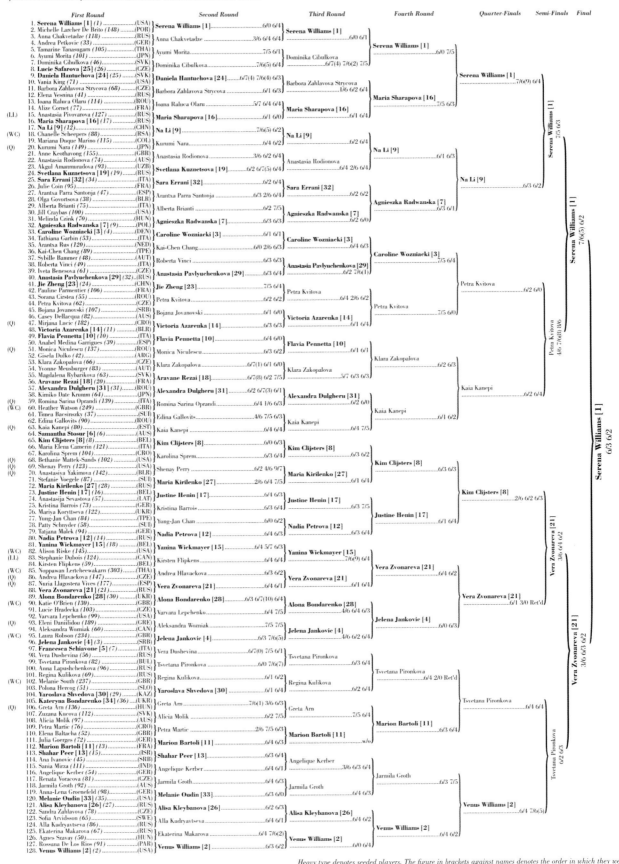

EVENT IV – THE LADIES' DOUBLES CHAMPIONSHIP 2010
HOLDERS: SERENA WILLIAMS & VENUS WILLIAMS

The Winners became the holders, for the year only, of the CHALLENGE CUPS presented by H.R.H. PRINCESS MARINA, DUCHESS OF KENT, the late President of The All England Lawn Tennis and Croquet Club in 1949 and The All England Lawn Tennis and Croquet Club in 2001. The Winners received a silver replica of the Challenge Cup. A Silver Salver was presented to each of the Runners-up and a Bronze Medal to each defeated Semi-finalist. The matches were the best of three sets.

First Round	Second Round	Third Round	Quarter-Finals	Semi-Finals	Final

1. **Serena Williams** (USA) & **Venus Williams** (USA)................**[1]**
   Serena Williams & Venus Williams [1]
2. Julie Ditty (USA) & Renata Voracova (CZE) 6/4 6/2
3. Tatjana Malek (GER) & Andrea Petkovic (GER) ....
   Timea Bacsinszky & Tathiana Garbin 6/4 6/4
4. Timea Bacsinszky (SUI) & Tathiana Garbin (ITA) ....

Serena Williams & Venus Williams [1] 6/1 7/6(2)

5. Dominika Cibulkova (SVK) & Anastasia Pavlyuchenkova (RUS) ....
   Dominika Cibulkova & Anastasia Pavlyuchenkova 4/6 6/2 6/1
6. Edina Gallovits (ROU) & Klaudia Jans (POL) ....
7. Julie Coin (FRA) & Marie-Eve Pelletier (CAN) ....
   Alicja Rosolska & Zi Yan [15] 6/3 6/2
8. **Alicja Rosolska** (POL) & **Zi Yan** (CHN) ....**[15]**

Dominika Cibulkova & Anastasia Pavlyuchenkova 7/5 6/1

Serena Williams & Venus Williams [1] 6/1 6/2

9. **Iveta Benesova** (CZE) & **Barbora Zahlavova Strycova** (CZE) ...**[12]**
   Iveta Benesova & Barbora Zahlavova Strycova [12] 6/2 5/7 6/2
(Q) 10. Eleni Daniilidou (GRE) & Jasmin Woehr (GER) ....
(WC) 11. Naomi Broady (GBR) & Katie O'Brien (GBR) ....
    Andrea Hlavackova & Lucie Hradecka 6/2 6/3
12. Andrea Hlavackova (CZE) & Lucie Hradecka (CZE) ....

Iveta Benesova & Barbora Zahlavova Strycova [12] 6/3 6/3

13. Elena Vesnina (RUS) & Vera Zvonareva (RUS) ....
    Elena Vesnina & Vera Zvonareva 7/5 6/4
(Q) 14. Mariya Koryttseva (UKR) & Darya Kustova (BLR) ....
15. Victoria Azarenka (BLR) & Anna Chakvetadze (RUS) ....
    Chia-Jung Chuang & Olga Govortsova [17] 3/6 7/6(2) 6/2
16. **Chia-Jung Chuang** (TPE) & **Olga Govortsova** (BLR) ....**[17]**

Elena Vesnina & Vera Zvonareva 6/4 5/7 7/5

Elena Vesnina & Vera Zvonareva 6/3 6/2

Serena Williams & Venus Williams [1] 6/1 6/2 *(crossed)*

Elena Vesnina & Vera Zvonareva 3/6 6/3 6/4

17. **Gisela Dulko** (ARG) & **Flavia Pennetta** (ITA) ....**[4]**
    Gisela Dulko & Flavia Pennetta [4] 6/2 4/6 6/1
18. Anastasia Rodionova (AUS) & Arina Rodionova (RUS) ....
19. Regina Kulikova (RUS) & Anastasija Sevastova (LAT) ....
    Elena Baltacha & Olga Savchuk 6/3 6/3
20. Elena Baltacha (GBR) & Olga Savchuk (UKR) ....

Gisela Dulko & Flavia Pennetta [4] 6/7(2) 6/3 6/0

21. Anabel Medina Garrigues (ESP) & Ipek Senoglu (TUR) ....
    Jelena Jankovic & Chanelle Scheepers 6/4 6/2
22. Jelena Jankovic (SRB) & Chanelle Scheepers (RSA) ....
23. Kirsten Flipkens (BEL) & Yanina Wickmayer (BEL) ....
    Vera Dushevina & Ekaterina Makarova [13] 7/6(4) 6/3
24. **Vera Dushevina** (RUS) & **Ekaterina Makarova** (RUS) ...**[13]**

Jelena Jankovic & Chanelle Scheepers 7/6(4) 6/4

Gisela Dulko & Flavia Pennetta [4] w/o

25. **Yung-Jan Chan** (TPE) & **Jie Zheng** (CHN) ....**[9]**
    Akgul Amanmuradova & Kristina Barrois 6/3 2/6 6/4
26. Akgul Amanmuradova (UZB) & Kristina Barrois (GER) ....
27. Magdalena Rybarikova (SVK) & Klara Zakopalova (CZE) ....
    Magdalena Rybarikova & Klara Zakopalova 6/3 7/6(3)
28. Melinda Czink (HUN) & Arantxa Parra Santonja (ESP) ....

Akgul Amanmuradova & Kristina Barrois 6/4 6/2

29. Julia Goerges (GER) & Agnes Szavay (HUN) ....
    Julia Goerges & Agnes Szavay 4/6 6/4 6/1
(WC) 30. Naomi Cavaday (GBR) & Anna Smith (GBR) ....
31. Kimiko Date Krumm (JPN) & Tamarine Tanasugarn (THA) ....
    Kai-Chen Chang & Ayumi Morita 6/3 7/6(4)
(LL) 32. Kai-Chen Chang (TPE) & Ayumi Morita (JPN) ....

Julia Goerges & Agnes Szavay 6/2 7/5

Julia Goerges & Agnes Szavay 6/2 7/6(7)

Gisela Dulko & Flavia Pennetta [4] 6/2 6/2

33. **Kveta Peschke** (CZE) & **Katarina Srebotnik** (SLO) ....**[6]**
    Kveta Peschke & Katarina Srebotnik [6] 6/2 7/5
(Q) 34. Jill Craybas (USA) & Marina Erakovic (NZL) ....
35. Ekaterina Dzehalevich (BLR) & Tatiana Poutchek (BLR) ....
    Virginia Ruano Pascual & Meghann Shaughnessy 6/4 7/5
36. Virginia Ruano Pascual (ESP) & Meghann Shaughnessy (USA) ...

Kveta Peschke & Katarina Srebotnik [6] 6/3 6/1

37. Natalie Grandin (RSA) & Abigail Spears (USA) ....
    Sara Errani & Roberta Vinci 6/3 6/3
38. Sara Errani (ITA) & Roberta Vinci (ITA) ....
39. Sofia Arvidsson (SWE) & Angelique Kerber (GER) ....
    Maria Kirilenko & Agnieszka Radwanska [10] 6/4 7/5
40. **Maria Kirilenko** (RUS) & **Agnieszka Radwanska** (POL) ...**[10]**

Sara Errani & Roberta Vinci 6/4 6/1

Kveta Peschke & Katarina Srebotnik [6] 7/5 6/3

41. **Monica Niculescu** (ROU) & **Shahar Peer** (ISR) ....**[14]**
    Monica Niculescu & Shahar Peer [14] 6/2 6/2
42. Alona Bondarenko (UKR) & Kateryna Bondarenko (UKR) ....
43. Vania King (USA) & Yaroslava Shvedova (KAZ) ....
    Vania King & Yaroslava Shvedova 6/1 6/2
44. Alberta Brianti (ITA) & Alexandra Dulgheru (ROU) ....

Vania King & Yaroslava Shvedova 6/0 3/6 6/2

45. Svetlana Kuznetsova (RUS) & Aravane Rezai (FRA) ....
    Svetlana Kuznetsova & Aravane Rezai 6/3 4/6 6/2
46. Liga Dekmeijere (LAT) & Petra Kvitova (CZE) ....
47. Melanie Oudin (USA) & Riza Zalameda (USA) ....
    Nadia Petrova & Samantha Stosur [3] 7/6(5) 6/0
48. **Nadia Petrova** (RUS) & **Samantha Stosur** (AUS) ....**[3]**

Nadia Petrova & Samantha Stosur [3] 6/0 6/4

Vania King & Yaroslava Shvedova 6/4 6/4

49. **Lisa Raymond** (USA) & **Rennae Stubbs** (AUS) ....**[7]**
    Lisa Raymond & Rennae Stubbs [7] 7/6(11) 4/6 6/4
50. Polona Hercog (SLO) & Petra Martic (CRO) ....
(WC) 51. Jocelyn Rae (GBR) & Heather Watson (GBR) ....
    Jocelyn Rae & Heather Watson 3/6 6/1 6/4
52. Casey Dellacqua (AUS) & Alicia Molik (AUS) ....

Lisa Raymond & Rennae Stubbs [7] 6/4 6/4

53. Sania Mirza (IND) & Caroline Wozniacki (DEN) ....
    Sania Mirza & Caroline Wozniacki 6/4 6/1
(WC) 54. Anne Keothavong (GBR) & Melanie South (GBR) ....
55. Maria Kondratieva (RUS) & Vladimira Uhlirova (CZE) ....
    Cara Black & Daniela Hantuchova [11] 6/2 2/6 6/2
56. **Cara Black** (ZIM) & **Daniela Hantuchova** (SVK) ....**[11]**

Cara Black & Daniela Hantuchova [11] 7/6(0) 6/3

Lisa Raymond & Rennae Stubbs [7] 6/2 6/2

57. **Su-Wei Hsieh** (TPE) & **Alla Kudryavtseva** (RUS) ....**[16]**
    Su-Wei Hsieh & Alla Kudryavtseva [16] 6/3 6/2
58. Michaella Krajicek (NED) & Patty Schnyder (SUI) ....
(WC) 59. Sally Peers (AUS) & Laura Robson (GBR) ....
    Kaia Kanepi & Shuai Zhang 6/2 6/4
(Q) 60. Kaia Kanepi (EST) & Shuai Zhang (CHN) ....

Su-Wei Hsieh & Alla Kudryavtseva [16] 6/3 4/6 6/1

61. Lucie Safarova (CZE) & Aleksandra Wozniak (CAN) ....
    Lucie Safarova & Aleksandra Wozniak 4/6 6/4 6/3
(LL) 62. Katalin Marosi (HUN) & Kathrin Woerle (GER) ....
63. Sarah Borwell (GBR) & Raquel Kops-Jones (USA) ....
    Liezel Huber & Bethanie Mattek-Sands [5] 6/1 6/1
64. **Liezel Huber** (USA) & **Bethanie Mattek-Sands** (USA) ...**[5]**

Liezel Huber & Bethanie Mattek-Sands [5] 6/7(1) 6/3 7/5

Liezel Huber & Bethanie Mattek-Sands [5] 3/6 6/2 6/2

Liezel Huber & Bethanie Mattek-Sands [5] 6/4 6/3

Vania King & Yaroslava Shvedova 6/4 6/4

Right-side later rounds (vertical text)

Serena Williams & Venus Williams [1] 6/1 6/2

Elena Vesnina & Vera Zvonareva 3/6 6/3 6/4

Elena Vesnina & Vera Zvonareva 6/3 6/2

Gisela Dulko & Flavia Pennetta [4] 6/2 6/2

Elena Vesnina & Vera Zvonareva 6/3 6/1

Vania King & Yaroslava Shvedova 3/6 7/5 6/3

Vania King & Yaroslava Shvedova 6/4 6/4

Vania King & Yaroslava Shvedova 7/6(6) 6/2

Heavy type denotes seeded players. The figure in brackets against names denotes the order in which they were seeded. (WC)=Wild card. (Q)=Qualifier. (LL)=Lucky loser.

EVENT V – THE MIXED DOUBLES CHAMPIONSHIP 2010
HOLDERS: MARK KNOWLES & ANNA-LENA GROENEFELD

The Winners became the holders, for the year only, of the CHALLENGE CUPS presented by members of the family of the late Mr. S. H. SMITH in 1949 and The All England Lawn Tennis and Croquet Club in 2001. The Winners received a silver replica of the Challenge Cup. A Silver Salver was presented to each of the Runners-up and a Bronze Medal to each defeated Semi-finalist. The matches were the best of three sets.

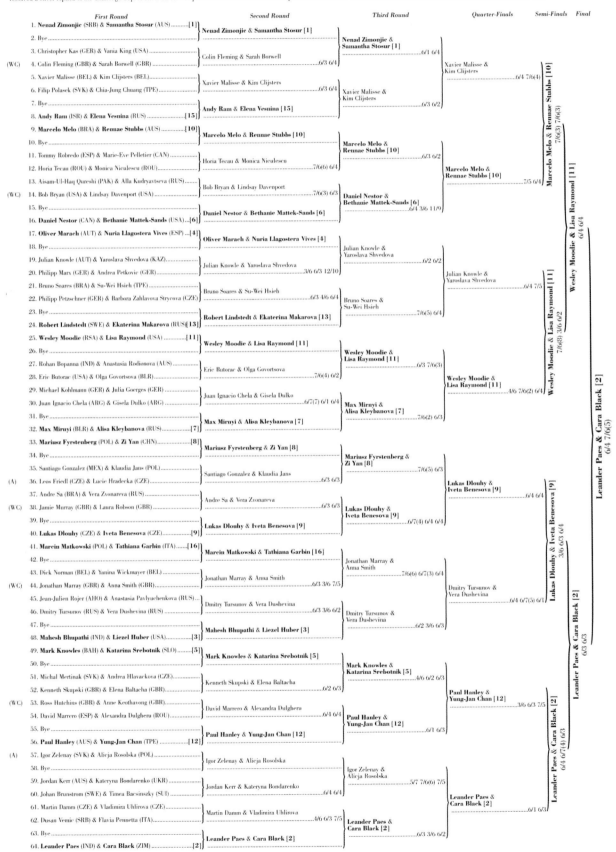

EVENT VI – THE GENTLEMEN'S INVITATION DOUBLES 2010
HOLDERS: JACCO ELTINGH & PAUL HAARHUIS

The Winners became the holders, for the year only, of a cup presented by The All England Lawn Tennis and Croquet Club. The Winners received miniature silver salvers. A silver medal was presented to each of the Runners-up. The matches were the best of three sets. If a match reached one set all a 10 point tie-break replaced the third set.

GROUP A	Jonas Bjorkman (SWE) & Todd Woodbridge (AUS)	Wayne Ferreira (RSA) & Yevgeny Kafelnikov (RUS)	Richard Krajicek (NED) & Michael Stich (GER)	Justin Gimelstob (USA) & Todd Martin (USA)	WINS	LOSSES	FINAL
Jonas Bjorkman (SWE) & Todd Woodbridge (AUS)		6/3 3/6 [10/12] L	6/3 7/6(6) W	5/0 Ret'd W	2	1	
Wayne Ferreira (RSA) & Yevgeny Kafelnikov (RUS)	3/6 6/3 [12/10] W		7/6(4) 4/6 [10/7]	4/6 5/7 L	2	1	Wayne Ferreira & Yevgeny Kafelnikov
Richard Krajicek (NED) & Michael Stich (GER)	3/6 6/7(6) L	6/7(4) 6/4 [7/10] L		7/6(5) 6/3 W	1	2	
Justin Gimelstob (USA) & Todd Martin (USA)	0/5 Ret'd L	6/4 7/5 W	6/7(5) 3/6 L		1	2	

Justin Gimelstob replaced Greg Rusedski after the first match.

GROUP B	Jacco Eltingh (NED) & Paul Haarhuis (NED)	Goran Ivanisevic (CRO) & Cedric Pioline (FRA)	Donald Johnson (USA) & Jared Palmer (USA)	Mark Petchey (GBR) & Chris Wilkinson (GBR)	WINS	LOSSES	FINAL
Jacco Eltingh (NED) & Paul Haarhuis (NED)		6/4 6/3 W	4/6 6/7(5) L	6/3 7/6(4) W	2	1	
Goran Ivanisevic (CRO) & Cedric Pioline (FRA)	4/6 3/6 L		7/6(4) 6/7(3) [5/10] L	6/4 7/6(4) W	1	2	Donald Johnson & Jared Palmer
Donald Johnson (USA) & Jared Palmer (USA)	6/4 7/6(5) W	6/7(4) 7/6(3) [10/5] W		6/3 7/6(3) W	3	0	
Mark Petchey (GBR) & Chris Wilkinson (GBR)	3/6 6/7(4) L	4/6 6/7(4) L	3/6 6/7(3) L		0	3	

FINAL: Donald Johnson & Jared Palmer 6/3 6/2

This event was played on a 'round robin' basis. 8 invited pairs were divided into 2 groups and each pair in each group played one another.
The pairs winning most matches were the winners of their respective groups and played a final round as indicated above.
If matches were equal in any group, the head to head result between the two pairs with the same number of wins, determined the winning pair of the group.
If that did not split the ties, then the percentage of sets won to sets played decided.

EVENT VII – THE GENTLEMEN'S SENIOR INVITATION DOUBLES 2010
HOLDERS: HOLDERS: JEREMY BATES & ANDERS JARRYD

The Winners became the holders, for the year only, of a Cup presented by The All England Lawn Tennis and Croquet Club. The Winners received miniature silver salvers. A Silver Medal was presented to each of the Runners-up. The matches were the best of three sets. If a match reached one set all a 10 point tie-break replaced the third set.

GROUP A	Mansour Bahrami (IRI) & Henri Leconte (FRA)	Jeremy Bates (GBR) & Anders Jarryd (SWE)	Peter Fleming (USA) & Guy Forget (FRA)	Joakim Nystrom (SWE) & Mikael Pernfors (SWE)	WINS	LOSSES	FINAL
Mansour Bahrami (IRI) & Henri Leconte (FRA)		2/6 2/6 L	3/6 6/3 [10/12] L	7/6(2) 7/6(5) W	1	2	
Jeremy Bates (GBR) & Anders Jarryd (SWE)	6/2 6/2 W		6/4 0/6 [10/8] W	W/O W	3	0	Jeremy Bates & Anders Jarryd
Peter Fleming (USA) & Guy Forget (FRA)	6/3 3/6 [12/10] W	4/6 6/0 [8/10] L		7/5 6/3 W	2	1	
Joakim Nystrom (SWE) & Mikael Pernfors (SWE)	6/7(2) 6/7(5) L	W/O L	5/7 3/6 L		0	3	

GROUP B	Vijay Amritraj (IND) & John Fitzgerald (AUS)	Pat Cash (AUS) & Mark Woodforde (AUS)	Kevin Curren (USA) & Johan Kriek (USA)	Peter McNamara (AUS) & Paul McNamee (AUS)	WINS	LOSSES	FINAL
Vijay Amritraj (IND) & John Fitzgerald (AUS)		3/6 4/6 L	3/6 4/6 L	3/6 2/6 L	0	3	
Pat Cash (AUS) & Mark Woodforde (AUS)	6/3 6/4 W		6/1 6/2 W	6/3 7/6(4) W	3	0	Pat Cash & Mark Woodforde
Kevin Curren (USA) & Johan Kriek (USA)	6/3 6/4 W	1/6 2/6 L		6/4 6/3 W	2	1	
Peter McNamara (AUS) & Paul McNamee (AUS)	6/3 6/2 W	3/6 6/7(4) L	4/6 3/6 L		1	2	

FINAL: Pat Cash & Mark Woodforde 6/2 7/6(5)

This event was played on a 'round robin' basis. 8 invited pairs were divided into 2 groups and each pair in each group played one another.
The pairs winning most matches were the winners of their respective groups and played a final round as indicated above.
If matches were equal in any group, the head to head result between the two pairs with the same number of wins, determined the winning pair of the group.
If that did not split the ties, then the percentage of sets won to sets played decided.

ALPHABETICAL LIST – INVITATION DOUBLES EVENTS

GENTLEMEN

Cash P. (Australia)
Eltingh J. (Netherlands)
Ferreira W. (South Africa)
Forget G. (France)

Haarhuis P. (Netherlands)
Jensen L. (USA)
Jensen M. (USA)
Johnson D. (USA)

Middleton T.J. (USA)
Palmer J. (USA)
Petchey M. (Great Britain)
Pioline C. (France)

Wheaton D. (USA)
Wilkinson C. (Great Britain)
Woodbridge T.A. (Australia)
Woodforde M. (Australia)

LADIES

Appelmans Miss S. (Belgium)
Bassett-Seguso Mrs C. (Canada)
Bollegraf Miss M.M. (Netherlands)
Croft Miss A. (Great Britain)

Durie Miss J.M. (Great Britain)
Kloss Miss I. (South Africa)
Magers Mrs G. (USA)
Mandlikova Miss H. (Australia)

Martinez Miss C. (Spain)
Navratilova Miss M. (USA)
Nideffer Mrs R.D. (USA)
Novotna Miss J. (Czech Republic)

Rinaldi Mrs K. (USA)
Smylie Mrs E.M. (Australia)
Sukova Miss H. (Czech Republic)
Tauziat Miss N. (France)

EVENT VIII – THE LADIES' INVITATION DOUBLES 2010
HOLDERS: MARTINA NAVRATILOVA & HELENA SUKOVA

The Winners became the holders, for the year only, of a Cup presented by The All England Lawn Tennis and Croquet Club. The Winners received miniature Cups.
A Silver Medal was presented to each of the Runners-up. The matches were the best of three sets. If a match reached one set all a 10 point tie-break replaced the third set.

GROUP A	Tracy Austin (USA) & Kathy Rinaldi-Stunkel (USA)	Martina Hingis (SUI) & Anna Kournikova (RUS)	Anne Hobbs (GBR) & Samantha Smith (GBR)	Helena Sukova (CZE) & Andrea Temesvari (HUN)	WINS	LOSSES	FINAL
Tracy Austin (USA) & Kathy Rinaldi-Stunkel (USA)		7/5 7/6(4) W	6/2 6/1 W	6/4 6/2 W	3	0	
Martina Hingis (SUI) & Anna Kournikova (RUS)	5/7 6/7(4) L		6/2 6/4 W	6/1 6/4 W	2	1	Tracy Austin & Kathy Rinaldi-Stunkel
Anne Hobbs (GBR) & Samantha Smith (GBR)	2/6 1/6 L	2/6 4/6 L		5/7 2/6 L	0	3	
Helena Sukova (CZE) & Andrea Temesvari (HUN)	4/6 2/6 L	1/6 4/6 L	7/5 6/2 W		1	2	

GROUP B	Annabel Croft (GBR) & Magdalena Maleeva (BUL)	Ilana Kloss (RSA) & Rosalyn Nideffer (USA)	Conchita Martinez (ESP) & Nathalie Tauziat (FRA)	Martina Navratilova (USA) & Jana Novotna (CZE)	WINS	LOSSES	
Annabel Croft (GBR) & Magdalena Maleeva (BUL)		6/4 6/1 W	4/6 4/6 L	6/7(4) 2/6 L	1	2	
Ilana Kloss (RSA) & Rosalyn Nideffer (USA)	4/6 1/6 L		4/6 1/6 L	3/6 1/6 L	0	3	Martina Navratilova & Jana Novotna
Conchita Martinez (ESP) & Nathalie Tauziat (FRA)	6/4 6/4 W	6/4 6/1 W		5/7 1/6 L	2	1	
Martina Navratilova (USA) & Jana Novotna (CZE)	7/6(4) 6/2 W	6/3 6/1 W	7/5 6/1 W		3	0	

FINAL: Martina Navratilova & Jana Novotna 7/5 6/0

This event will be played on a 'round robin' basis. 8 invited pairs have been divided into 2 groups of 4 and each pair in each group will play one another. The pairs winning most matches will be the winners of their respective groups and will play a final round as indicated above. If matches should be equal in any group, the head to head result between the two pairs with the same number of wins will determine the winning pair of the group.

EVENT IX – THE WHEELCHAIR GENTLEMEN'S DOUBLES 2010
HOLDERS: STEPHANE HOUDET & MICHAEL JEREMIASZ

The Winners received Silver Salvers. The matches were the best of three tie-break sets.

Third & Fourth Place Play-off	First Round	Final
	1. **Stephane Houdet** (FRA) & **Shingo Kunieda** (JPN) ....[1]	
Frederic Cattaneo (FRA) & Nicolas Peifer (FRA)		Stephane Houdet & Shingo Kunieda [1]
	2. Frederic Cattaneo (FRA) & Nicolas Peifer (FRA)	...........6/3 6/2
	3. Robin Ammerlaan (NED) & Stefan Olsson (SWE)	
Maikel Scheffers & Ronald Vink [2]		Robin Ammerlaan & Stefan Olsson
	4. **Maikel Scheffers** (NED) & **Ronald Vink** (NED) ....[2]	...........7/6(5) 6/2

Maikel Scheffers & Ronald Vink [2] 6/1 6/4

Robin Ammerlaan & Stefan Olsson 6/4 7/6(4)

EVENT X – THE WHEELCHAIR LADIES' DOUBLES 2010
HOLDERS: KORIE HOMAN & ESTHER VERGEER

The Winners received Silver Salvers. The matches were the best of three tie-break sets.

Third & Fourth Place Play-off	First Round	Final
	1. **Esther Vergeer** (NED) & **Sharon Walraven** (NED) ....[1]	
Annick Sevenans & Aniek Van Koot		**Esther Vergeer & Sharon Walraven [1]**
	2. Annick Sevenans (BEL) & Aniek Van Koot (NED)	...........6/0 6/3
	3. Daniela Di Toro (AUS) & Lucy Shuker (GBR)	
Florence Alix-Gravellier & Jiske Griffioen		Daniela Di Toro & Lucy Shuker
	4. **Florence Alix-Gravellier** (FRA) & **Jiske Griffioen** (NED) ...[2]	...........7/6(4) 3/6 6/3

Annick Sevenans & Aniek Van Koot 6/3 6/7(2) 6/4

Esther Vergeer & Sharon Walraven [1] 6/2 6/3

ALPHABETICAL LIST – GENTLEMEN'S SENIOR INVITATION DOUBLES EVENT

Amritraj V. *(India)*
Bahrami M. *(Iran)*
Bates M.J. *(Great Britain)*
Curren K. *(USA)*

Fitzgerald J.B. *(Australia)*
Flach K. *(USA)*
Fleming P. *(USA)*
Guenthardt H. *(Switzerland)*

Jarryd A. *(Sweden)*
Leconte H. *(France)*
Mayer G. *(USA)*
McNamara P. *(Australia)*

McNamee P.F. *(Australia)*
Seguso R. *(USA)*
Taroczy B. *(Hungary)*
Vilas G. *(Argentina)*

EVENT XI – THE BOYS' SINGLES CHAMPIONSHIP 2010
HOLDER: ANDREY KUZNETSOV

The Winner became the holder, for the year only, of a Cup presented by The All England Lawn Tennis and Croquet Club. The Winner received a miniature Cup and the Runner-up received a memento. The matches were best of three sets.

Heavy type denotes seeded players. The figure in brackets against names denotes the order in which they were seeded.
(WC)=Wild card. (Q)=Qualifier.

EVENT XII – THE BOYS' DOUBLES CHAMPIONSHIP 2010
HOLDERS: PIERRE-HUGUES HERBERT & KEVIN KRAWIETZ

The Winners became the holders, for the year only, of a Cup presented by The All England Lawn Tennis and Croquet Club.
The Winners received miniature Cups and the Runners-up received mementos. The matches were best of three sets.

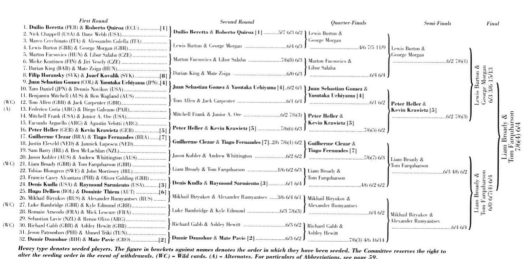

Heavy type denotes seeded players. The figure in brackets against names denotes the order in which they have been seeded. The Committee reserves the right to alter the seeding order in the event of withdrawals. (WC) = Wild cards. (A) = Alternates. For particulars of Abbreviations, see page 59.

Heavy type denotes seeded players. The figure in brackets against names denotes the order in which they were seeded.
(WC)=Wild card. (A)=Alternates

EVENT XIII – THE GIRLS' SINGLES CHAMPIONSHIP 2010
HOLDER: NOPPAWAN LERTCHEEWAKARN

The Winner became the holder, for the year only, of a Cup presented by The All England Lawn Tennis and Croquet Club.
The Winner received a miniature Cup and the Runner-up received a memento. The matches were best of three sets.

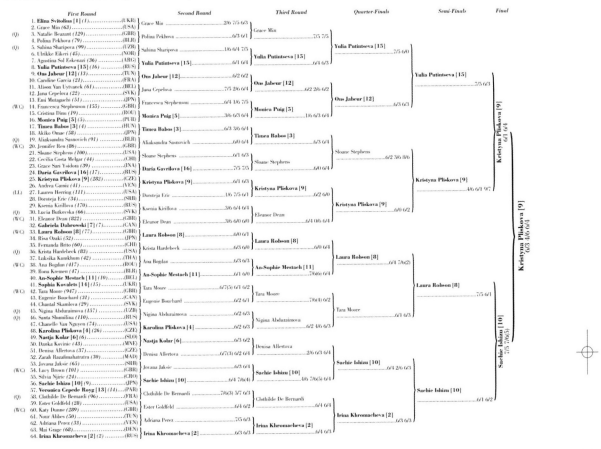

Heavy type denotes seeded players. The figure in brackets against names denotes the order in which they were seeded.
(WC)=Wild card. (Q)=Qualifier. (LL)=Lucky Loser.

EVENT XIV – THE GIRLS' DOUBLES CHAMPIONSHIP 2010
HOLDERS: NOPPAWAN LERTCHEEWAKARN & SALLY PEERS

The Winners became the holders, for the year only, of a Cup presented by The All England Lawn Tennis and Croquet Club.
The Winners received miniature Cups and the Runners-up received mementoes. The matches were best of three sets.

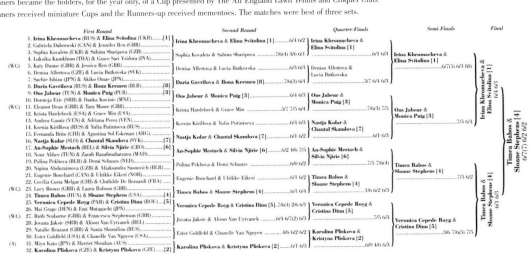

Heavy type denotes seeded players. The figure in brackets against names denotes the order in which they were seeded.
(A)=Alternates. (WC)=Wild card.

1877	S. W. Gore *W. C. Marshall*	1902	H. L. Doherty *A. W. Gore*	* 1931	S. B. Wood *F. X. Shields*	1962	R. Laver *M. F. Mulligan*	1987	P. Cash *I. Lendl*
1878	P. F. Hadow *S. W. Gore*	1903	H. L. Doherty *F. L. Riseley*	1932	H. E. Vines *H. W. Austin*	* 1963	C. R. McKinley *F. S. Stolle*	1988	S. Edberg *B. Becker*
* 1879	J. T. Hartley *V. St. L. Goold*	1904	H. L. Doherty *F. L. Riseley*	1933	J. H. Crawford *H. E. Vines*	1964	R. Emerson *F. S. Stolle*	1989	B. Becker *S. Edberg*
1880	J. T. Hartley *H. F. Lawford*	1905	H. L. Doherty *N. E. Brookes*	1934	F. J. Perry *J. H. Crawford*	1965	R. Emerson *F. S. Stolle*	1990	S. Edberg *B. Becker*
1881	W. Renshaw *J. T. Hartley*	1906	H. L. Doherty *F. L. Riseley*	1935	F. J. Perry *G. von Cramm*	1966	M. Santana *R. D. Ralston*	1991	M. Stich *B. Becker*
1882	W. Renshaw *E. Renshaw*	* 1907	N. E. Brookes *A. W. Gore*	1936	F. J. Perry *G. von Cramm*	1967	J. D. Newcombe *W. P. Bungert*	1992	A. Agassi *G. Ivanisevic*
1883	W. Renshaw *E. Renshaw*	* 1908	A. W. Gore *H. Roper Barrett*	* 1937	J. D. Budge *G. von Cramm*	1968	R. Laver *A. D. Roche*	1993	P. Sampras *J. Courier*
1884	W. Renshaw *H. F. Lawford*	1909	A. W. Gore *M. J. G. Ritchie*	1938	J. D. Budge *H. W. Austin*	1969	R. Laver *J. D. Newcombe*	1994	P. Sampras *G. Ivanisevic*
1885	W. Renshaw *H. F. Lawford*	1910	A. F. Wilding *A. W. Gore*	* 1939	R. L. Riggs *E. T. Cooke*	1970	J. D. Newcombe *K. R. Rosewall*	1995	P. Sampras *B. Becker*
1886	W. Renshaw *H. F. Lawford*	1911	A. F. Wilding *H. Roper Barrett*	* 1946	Y. Petra *G. E. Brown*	1971	J. D. Newcombe *S. R. Smith*	1996	R. Krajicek *M. Washington*
* 1887	H. F. Lawford *E. Renshaw*	1912	A. F. Wilding *A. W. Gore*	1947	J. Kramer *T. Brown*	* 1972	S. R. Smith *I. Nastase*	1997	P. Sampras *C. Pioline*
1888	E. Renshaw *H. F. Lawford*	1913	A. F. Wilding *M. E. McLoughlin*	* 1948	R. Falkenburg *J. E. Bromwich*	* 1973	J. Kodes *A. Metreveli*	1998	P. Sampras *G. Ivanisevic*
1889	W. Renshaw *E. Renshaw*	1914	N. E. Brookes *A. F. Wilding*	1949	F. R. Schroeder *J. Drobny*	1974	J. S. Connors *K. R. Rosewall*	1999	P. Sampras *A. Agassi*
1890	W. J. Hamilton *W. Renshaw*	1919	G. L. Patterson *N. E. Brookes*	* 1950	B. Patty *F. A. Sedgman*	1975	A. R. Ashe *J. S. Connors*	2000	P. Sampras *P. Rafter*
* 1891	W. Baddeley *J. Pim*	1920	W. T. Tilden *G. L. Patterson*	1951	R. Savitt *K. McGregor*	1976	B. Borg *I. Nastase*	2001	G. Ivanisevic *P. Rafter*
1892	W. Baddeley *J. Pim*	1921	W. T. Tilden *B. I. C. Norton*	1952	F. A. Sedgman *J. Drobny*	1977	B. Borg *J. S. Connors*	2002	L. Hewitt *D. Nalbandian*
1893	J. Pim *W. Baddeley*	*† 1922	G. L. Patterson *R. Lycett*	* 1953	V. Seixas *K. Nielsen*	1978	B. Borg *J. S.Connors*	2003	R. Federer *M. Philippoussis*
1894	J. Pim *W. Baddeley*	* 1923	W. M. Johnston *F. T. Hunter*	1954	J. Drobny *K. R. Rosewall*	1979	B. Borg *R. Tanner*	2004	R. Federer *A. Roddick*
* 1895	W. Baddeley *W. V. Eaves*	* 1924	J. Borotra *R. Lacoste*	1955	T. Trabert *K. Nielsen**	1980	B. Borg *J. P. McEnroe*	2005	R. Federer *A. Roddick*
1896	H. S. Mahony *W. Baddeley*	1925	R. Lacoste *J. Borotra*	1956	L. A. Hoad *K. R. Rosewall*	1981	J. P. McEnroe *B. Borg*	2006	R. Federer *R. Nadal*
1897	R. F. Doherty *H. S. Mahony*	* 1926	J. Borotra *H. Kinsey*	1957	L. A. Hoad *A. J. Cooper*	1982	J. S. Connors *J. P. McEnroe*	2007	R. Federer *R. Nadal*
1898	R. F. Doherty *H. L . Doherty*	1927	H. Cochet *J. Borotra*	* 1958	A. J. Cooper *N. A. Fraser*	1983	J. P. McEnroe *C. J. Lewis*	2008	R. Nadal *R. Federer*
1899	R. F. Doherty *A. W. Gore*	1928	R. Lacoste *H. Cochet*	* 1959	A. Olmedo *R. Laver*	1984	J. P. McEnroe *J. S. Connors*	2009	R. Federer *A. Roddick*
1900	R. F. Doherty *S. H. Smith*	* 1929	H. Cochet *J. Borotra*	* 1960	N. A. Fraser *R. Laver*	1985	B. Becker *K. Curren*	2010	R. Nadal *T. Berdych*
1901	A. W. Gore *R. F. Doherty*	1930	W. T. Tilden *W. Allison*	1961	R. Laver *C. R. McKinley*	1986	B.Becker *I. Lendl*		

For the years 1913, 1914 and 1919-1923 inclusive the above records include the "World's Championships on Grass" granted to The Lawn Tennis Association by The International Lawn Tennis Federation.
This title was then abolished and commencing in 1924 they became The Official Lawn Tennis Championships recognised by The International Lawn Tennis Federation.
Prior to 1922 the holders in the Singles Events and Gentlemen's Doubles did not compete in the Championships but met the winners of these events in the Challenge Rounds.
*† Challenge Round abolished; holders subsequently played through. * The holder did not defend the title.*

THE CHAMPIONSHIP ROLL
LADIES' SINGLES—CHAMPIONS & RUNNERS UP

1884 Miss M. Watson
Miss L. Watson

1885 Miss M. Watson
Miss B. Bingley

1886 Miss B. Bingley
Miss M. Watson

1887 Miss L. Dod
Miss B. Bingley

1888 Miss L. Dod
Mrs. G. W. Hillyard

* 1889 Mrs. G. W. Hillyard
Miss L. Rice

* 1890 Miss L. Rice
Miss M. Jacks

* 1891 Miss L. Dod
Mrs. G. W. Hillyard

1892 Miss L. Dod
Mrs. G. W. Hillyard

1893 Miss L. Dod
Mrs. G. W. Hillyard

* 1894 Mrs. G. W. Hillyard
Miss E. L. Austin

* 1895 Miss C. Cooper
Miss H. Jackson

1896 Miss C. Cooper
Mrs. W. H.Pickering

1897 Mrs. G. W. Hillyard
Miss C. Cooper

* 1898 Miss C. Cooper
Miss L Martin

1899 Mrs. G. W. Hillyard
Miss C. Cooper

1900 Mrs. G. W. Hillyard
Miss C. Cooper

1901 Mrs. A. Sterry
Mrs. G. W. Hillyard

1902 Miss M. E. Robb
Mrs. A. Sterry

* 1903 Miss D. K. Douglass
Miss E. W. Thomson

1904 Miss D. K. Douglass
Mrs. A. Sterry

1905 Miss M. Sutton
Miss D. K. Douglass

1906 Miss D. K. Douglass
Miss M. Sutton

1907 Miss M. Sutton
Mrs. Lambert Chambers

* 1908 Mrs. A. Sterry
Miss A. M. Morton

* 1909 Miss D. P. Boothby
Miss A. M. Morton

1910 Mrs. Lambert Chambers
Miss D. P. Boothby

1911 Mrs. Lambert Chambers
Miss D. P. Boothby

* 1912 Mrs. D. R. Larcombe
Mrs. A. Sterry

* 1913 Mrs. Lambert Chambers
Mrs. R. J. McNair

1914 Mrs. Lambert Chambers
Mrs. D. R. Larcombe

1919 Miss S. Lenglen
Mrs. Lambert Chambers

1920 Miss S. Lenglen
Mrs. Lambert Chambers

1921 Miss S. Lenglen
Miss E. Ryan

† 1922 Miss S. Lenglen
Mrs. F. Mallory

1923 Miss S. Lenglen
Miss K. McKane

1924 Miss K. McKane
Miss H. Wills

1925 Miss S. Lenglen
Miss J. Fry

1926 Mrs. L. A. Godfree
Miss L. de Alvarez

1927 Miss H. Wills
Miss L. de Alvarez

1928 Miss H. Wills
Miss L. de Alvarez

1929 Miss H. Wills
Miss H. H. Jacobs

1930 Mrs. F. S. Moody
Miss E. Ryan

* 1931 Miss C. Aussem
Miss H. Krahwinkel

* 1932 Mrs. F. S. Moody
Miss H. H. Jacobs

1933 Mrs. F. S. Moody
Miss D. E. Round

* 1934 Miss D. E. Round
Miss H. H. Jacobs

1935 Mrs. F. S. Moody
Miss H. H. Jacobs

* 1936 Miss H. H. Jacobs
Miss S. Sperling

1937 Mrs D. E. Round
Miss J. Jedrzejowska

* 1938 Mrs. F. S. Moody
Miss H. H. Jacobs

* 1939 Miss A. Marble
Miss K. E. Stammers

* 1946 Miss P. Betz
Miss L. Brough

* 1947 Miss M. Osborne
Miss D. Hart

1948 Miss L. Brough
Miss D. Hart

1949 Miss L. Brough
Mrs. W. du Pont

1950 Miss L. Brough
Mrs. W. du Pont

1951 Miss D. Hart
Miss S. Fry

1952 Miss M. Connolly
Miss L. Brough

1953 Miss M. Connolly
Miss D. Hart

1954 Miss M. Connolly
Miss L. Brough

* 1955 Miss L. Brough
Mrs. J. G. Fleitz

1956 Miss S. Fry
Miss A. Buxton

* 1957 Miss A. Gibson
Miss D. R. Hard

1958 Miss A. Gibson
Miss A. Mortimer

* 1959 Miss M. E. Bueno
Miss D. R. Hard

1960 Miss M. E. Bueno
Miss S. Reynolds

* 1961 Miss A. Mortimer
Miss C. C. Truman

1962 Mrs. J. R. Susman
Mrs. V. Sukova

* 1963 Miss M. Smith
Miss B. J. Moffitt

1964 Miss M. E. Bueno
Miss M. Smith

1965 Miss M. Smith
Miss M. E. Bueno

1966 Mrs. L. W. King
Miss M. E. Bueno

1967 Mrs. L. W. King
Mrs. P. F. Jones

1968 Mrs. L. W. King
Miss J. A. M. Tegart

1969 Mrs. P. F. Jones
Mrs. L. W. King

* 1970 Mrs. B. M. Court
Mrs. L. W. King

1971 Miss E. F. Goolagong
Mrs. B. M. Court

1972 Mrs. L. W. King
Miss E. F. Goolagong

1973 Mrs. L. W. King
Miss C. M. Evert

1974 Miss C. M. Evert
Mrs. O. Morozova

1975 Mrs. L. W. King
Mrs. R. Cawley

* 1976 Miss C. M. Evert
Mrs. R. Cawley

1977 Miss S. V. Wade
Miss B. F. Stove

1978 Miss M. Navratilova
Miss C. M. Evert

1979 Miss M. Navratilova
Mrs. J. M. Lloyd

1980 Mrs. R. Cawley
Mrs. J. M. Lloyd

* 1981 Mrs. J. M. Lloyd
Miss H. Mandlikova

1982 Miss M. Navratilova
Mrs. J. M. Lloyd

1983 Miss M. Navratilova
Miss A. Jaeger

1984 Miss M. Navratilova
Mrs. J. M. Lloyd

1985 Miss M. Navratilova
Mrs. J. M. Lloyd

1986 Miss M. Navratilova
Miss H. Mandlikova

1987 Miss M. Navratilova
Miss S. Graf

1988 Miss S. Graf
Miss M. Navratilova

1989 Miss S. Graf
Miss M. Navratilova

1990 Miss M. Navratilova
Miss Z. Garrison

1991 Miss S. Graf
Miss G. Sabatini

1992 Miss S. Graf
Miss M. Seles

1993 Miss S. Graf
Miss J. Novotna

1994 Miss C. Martinez
Miss M. Navratilova

1995 Miss S. Graf
Miss A. Sanchez Vicario

1996 Miss S. Graf
Miss A. Sanchez Vicario

* 1997 Miss M. Hingis
Miss J. Novotna

1998 Miss J. Novotna
Miss N. Tauziat

1999 Miss L.A. Davenport
Miss S. Graf

2000 Miss V. Williams
Miss L.A. Davenport

2001 Miss V. Williams
Miss J. Henin

2002 Miss S. Williams
Miss V. Williams

2003 Miss S. Williams
Miss V. Williams

2004 Miss M. Sharapova
Miss S. Williams

2005 Miss V. Williams
Miss L. Davenport

2006 Miss A. Mauresmo
Mrs J. Henin-Hardenne

2007 Miss V. Williams
Miss M. Bartoli

2008 Miss V. Williams
Miss S. Williams

2009 Miss S. Williams
Miss V. Williams

2010 Miss S. Williams
Miss V. Zvonareva

MAIDEN NAMES OF LADY CHAMPIONS *(In the tables the following have been recorded in both married and single identities)*

Mrs. R. Cawley..................Miss E. F. Goolagong	Mrs J. Henin-Hardenne ....Miss J. Henin	Mrs. O. Morozova ....Miss O. Morozova
Mrs. Lambert Chambers..................Miss D. K. Douglass	Mrs. G. W. Hillyard.........................Miss B. Bingley	Mrs. L. E. G. Price.........................Miss S. Reynolds
Mrs. B. M. Court..................Miss M. Smith	Mrs. P. F. Jones ....Miss A. S. Haydon	Mrs. G. E. Reid.............................Miss K. Melville
Mrs. B. C. Covell..................Miss P. L. Howkins	Mrs. L. W. King.............................Miss B. J. Moffitt	Mrs. P. D. Smylie...........................Miss E. M. Sayers
Mrs. D. E. Dalton..................Miss J. A. M. Tegart	Mrs. M. R. King..........................Miss P. E. Mudford	Frau. S. Sperling.......................Fraulein H. Krahwinkel
Mrs. W. du Pont ....Miss M. Osborne	Mrs. D. R. Larcombe......................Miss E. W. Thomson	Mrs. A. Sterry..............................Miss C. Cooper
Mrs. L. A. Godfree..................Miss K. McKane	Mrs. J. M. Lloyd ....Miss C. M. Evert	Mrs. J. R. Susman..........................Miss K. Hantze
Mrs. H. F. Gourlay Cawley ....Miss H. F. Gourlay	Mrs. F. S. Moody..........................Miss H. Wills	

THE CHAMPIONSHIP ROLL

GENTLEMEN'S DOUBLES—CHAMPIONS & RUNNERS UP

1879 L. R. Erskine and H. F. Lawford
F. Durant and G. E. Tabor

1880 W. Renshaw and E. Renshaw
O. E. Woodhouse and C. J. Cole

1881 W. Renshaw and E. Renshaw
W. J. Down and H. Vaughan

1882 J. T. Hartley and R. T. Richardson
J. G. Horn and C. B. Russell

1883 C. W. Grinstead and C. E. Welldon
C. B. Russell and R. T. Milford

1884 W. Renshaw and E. Renshaw
E. W. Lewis and E. L Williams

1885 W. Renshaw and E. Renshaw
C. E. Farrer and A. J. Stanley

1886 W. Renshaw and E. Renshaw
C. E. Farrer and A. J. Stanley

1887 P. Bowes-Lyon and H. W. W. Wilberforce
J. H. Crispe and E. Barratt Smith

1888 W. Renshaw and E. Renshaw
P Bowes-Lyon and H. W. W. Wilberforce

1889 W. Renshaw and E. Renshaw
E. W. Lewis and G. W. Hillyard

1890 J. Pim and F. O. Stoker
E. W. Lewis and G. W. Hillyard

1891 W. Baddeley and H. Baddeley
J. Pim and F. O. Stoker

1892 H. S. Barlow and E. W. Lewis
W. Baddeley and H. Baddeley

1893 J. Pim and F. O. Stoker
E. W. Lewis and H. S. Barlow

1894 W. Baddeley and H. Baddeley
H. S. Barlow and C. H. Martin

1895 W. Baddeley and H. Baddeley
E. W. Lewis and W. V. Eaves

1896 W. Baddeley and H. Baddeley
R. F. Doherty and H. A. Nisbet

1897 R. F. Doherty and H. L. Doherty
W. Baddeley and H. Baddeley

1898 R. F. Doherty and H. L . Doherty
H. A. Nisbet and C. Hobart

1899 R. F. Doherty and H. L. Doherty
H. A. Nisbet and C. Hobart

1900 R. F. Doherty and H. L. Doherty
H. Roper Barrett and H. A. Nisbet

1901 R. F. Doherty and H. L. Doherty
Dwight Davis and Holcombe Ward

1902 S. H. Smith and F. L. Riseley
R. F. Doherty and H. L. Doherty

1903 R. F. Doherty and H. L. Doherty
S. H. Smith and F. L. Riseley

1904 R. F. Doherty and H. L. Doherty
S. H. Smith and F. L. Riseley

1905 R. F. Doherty and H. L. Doherty
S. H. Smith and F. L. Riseley

1906 S. H. Smith and F. L. Riseley
R. F. Doherty and H. L. Doherty

1907 N. E. Brookes and A. F. Wilding
B. C. Wright and K. H. Behr

1908 A. F. Wilding and M. J. G. Ritchie
A. W. Gore and H. Roper Barrett

1909 A. W. Gore and H. Roper Barrett
S. N. Doust and H. A. Parker

1910 A. F. Wilding and M. J. G. Ritchie
A. W. Gore and H. Roper Barrett

1911 M. Decugis and A. H. Gobert
M. J. G. Ritchie and A. F. Wilding

1912 H. Roper Barrett and C. P. Dixon
M. Decugis and A. H. Gobert

1913 H. Roper Barrett and C. P. Dixon
F. W. Rahe and H. Kleinschroth

1914 N. E. Brookes and A. F. Wilding
H. Roper Barrett and C. P. Dixon

1919 R. V. Thomas and P. O'Hara-Wood
R. Lycett and R. W. Heath

1920 R. N. Williams and C. S. Garland
A. R. F. Kingscote and J. C. Parke

1921 R. Lycett and M. Woosnam
F. G. Lowe and A. H. Lowe

1922 R. Lycett and J. O. Anderson
G. L. Patterson and P. O'Hara-Wood

1923 R. Lycett and L. A. Godfree
Count de Gomar and E. Flaquer

1924 F. T. Hunter and V. Richards
R. N. Williams and W. M. Washburn

1925 J. Borotra and R. Lacoste
J. Hennessey and R. Casey

1926 H. Cochet and J. Brugnon
V. Richards and H. Kinsey

1927 F. T. Hunter and W. T. Tilden
J. Brugnon and H. Cochet

1928 H. Cochet and J. Brugnon
G. L. Patterson and J. B. Hawkes

1929 W. Allison and J. Van Ryn
J. C. Gregory and I. G. Collins

1930 W. Allison and J. Van Ryn
J. H. Doeg and G. M. Lott

1931 G. M Lott and J. Van Ryn
H. Cochet and J. Brugnon

1932 J. Borotra and J. Brugnon
G. P. Hughes and F. J. Perry

1933 J. Borotra and J. Brugnon
R. Nunoi and J. Satoh

1934 G. M. Lott and L. R. Stoefen
J. Borotra and J. Brugnon

1935 J. H. Crawford and A. K. Quist
W. Allison and J. Van Ryn

1936 G. P. Hughes and C. R. D. Tuckey
C. E. Hare and F. H. D. Wilde

1937 J. D. Budge and G. Mako
G. P. Hughes and C. R. D. Tuckey

1938 J. D. Budge and G. Mako
H. Henkel and G. von Metaxa

1939 R. L. Riggs and E. T. Cooke
C. E. Hare and F. H. D. Wilde

1946 T. Brown and J. Kramer
G. E. Brown and D. Pails

1947 R. Falkenburg and J. Kramer
A. J. Mottram and O. W. Sidwell

1948 J. E. Bromwich and F. A. Sedgman
T. Brown and G. Mulloy

1949 R. Gonzales and F. Parker
G. Mulloy and F. R. Schroeder

1950 J. E. Bromwich and A. K. Quist
G. E. Brown and O. W Sidwell

1951 K. McGregor and F. A. Sedgman
J. Drobny and E. W. Sturgess

1952 K. McGregor and F. A. Sedgman
V. Seixas and E. W. Sturgess

1953 L. A. Hoad and K. R. Rosewall
R. N. Hartwig and M. G. Rose

1954 R. N. Hartwig and M. G. Rose
V. Seixas and T. Trabert

1955 R. N. Hartwig and L. A. Hoad
N. A. Fraser and K. R. Rosewall

1956 L. A. Hoad and K. R. Rosewall
N. Pietrangeli and O. Sirola

1957 G. Mulloy and B. Patty
N. A. Fraser and L. A. Hoad

1958 S. Davidson and U. Schmidt
A. J. Cooper and N. A. Fraser

1959 R. Emerson and N. A. Fraser
R. Laver and R. Mark

1960 R. H. Osuna and R. D. Ralston
M. G. Davies and R. K. Wilson

1961 R. Emerson and N. A. Fraser
R. A. J. Hewitt and F. S. Stolle

1962 R. A. J. Hewitt and F. S. Stolle
B. Jovanovic and N. Pilic

1963 R. H. Osuna and A. Palafox
J. C. Barclay and P. Darmon

1964 R. A. J. Hewitt and F. S. Stolle
R. Emerson and K. N. Fletcher

1965 J. D. Newcombe and A. D. Roche
K. N. Fletcher and R. A. J. Hewitt

1966 K. N. Fletcher and J. D. Newcombe
W. W. Bowrey and O. K. Davidson

1967 R. A. J. Hewitt and F. D. McMillan
R. Emerson and K. N. Fletcher

1968 J. D. Newcombe and A. D. Roche
K. R. Rosewall and F. S. Stolle

1969 J. D. Newcombe and A. D. Roche
T. S. Okker and M. C. Reissen

1970 J. D. Newcombe and A. D. Roche
K. R. Rosewall and F. S. Stolle

1971 R. S. Emerson and R. G. Laver
A. R. Ashe and R. D. Ralston

1972 R. A. J. Hewitt and F. D. McMillan
S. R. Smith and E. J. van Dillen

1973 J. S. Connors and I. Nastase
J. R. Cooper and N. A. Fraser

1974 J. D. Newcombe and A. D. Roche
R. C. Lutz and S. R. Smith

1975 V. Gerulaitis and A. Mayer
C. Dowdeswell and A. J. Stone

1976 B. E. Gottfried and R. Ramirez
R. L. Case and G. Masters

1977 R. L. Case and G. Masters
J. G. Alexander and P. C. Dent

1978 R. A. J. Hewitt and F. D. McMillan
P. Fleming and J. P. McEnroe

1979 P. Fleming and J. P . McEnroe
B. E. Gottfried and R. Ramirez

1980 P. McNamara and P. McNamee
R. C. Lutz and S. R. Smith

1981 P. Fleming and J. P. McEnroe
R. C. Lutz and S. R. Smith

1982 P. McNamara and P. McNamee
P. Fleming and J. P. McEnroe

1983 P. Fleming and J. P McEnroe
T. E. Gullikson and T. R. Gullikson

1984 P. Fleming and J. P. McEnroe
P. Cash and P. McNamee

1985 H. P. Guenthardt and B. Taroczy
P. Cash and J. B. Fitzgerald

1986 J. Nystrom and M. Wilander
G. Donnelly and P. Fleming

1987 K. Flach and R. Seguso
S. Casal and E. Sanchez

1988 K. Flach and R. Seguso
J. B. Fitzgerald and A. Jarryd

1989 J. B. Fitzgerald and A. Jarryd
R. Leach and J. Pugh

1990 R. Leach and J. Pugh
P. Aldrich and D. T. Visser

1991 J. B. Fitzgerald and A. Jarryd
J. Frana and L. Lavalle

1992 J. P. McEnroe and M. Stich
J. Grabb and R. A. Reneberg

1993 T. A. Woodbridge and M. Woodforde
G. Connell and P. Galbraith

1994 T. A. Woodbridge and M. Woodforde
G. Connell and P. Galbraith

1995 T. A. Woodbridge and M. Woodforde
R. Leach and S. Melville

1996 T. A. Woodbridge and M. Woodforde
B. Black and G. Connell

1997 T. A. Woodbridge and M. Woodforde
J. Eltingh and P. Haarhuis

1998 J. Eltingh and P. Haarhuis
T. A. Woodbridge and M. Woodforde

1999 M. Bhupathi and L. Paes
P. Haarhuis and J. Palmer

2000 T. A. Woodbridge and M. Woodforde
P. Haarhuis and S. Stolle

2001 D. Johnson and J. Palmer
J. Novak and D. Rikl

2002 J. Bjorkman and T. A Woodbridge
M. Knowles and D. Nestor

2003 J. Bjorkman and T. A Woodbridge
M. Bhupathi and M. Mirnyi

2004 J. Bjorkman and T. A Woodbridge
J. Knowle and N. Zimonjic

2005 S. Huss and W. Moodie
B. Bryan and M. Bryan

2006 B. Bryan and M. Bryan
F. Santoro and N. Zimonjic

2007 A. Clement and M. Llodra
B. Bryan and M. Bryan

2008 D. Nestor and N. Zimonjic
J. Bjorkman and K. Ullyett

2009 D. Nestor and N. Zimonjic
B. Bryan and M. Bryan

2010 J. Melzer & P. Petzschner
R. Lindstedt & H. Tecau

LADIES' DOUBLES—CHAMPIONS & RUNNERS UP

1913 Mrs. R. J. McNair and Miss D. P. Boothby
Mrs. A. Sterry and Mrs. Lambert Chambers

1914 Miss E. Ryan and Miss A. M. Morton
Mrs. D. R. Larcombe and Mrs. F. J. Hannam

1919 Miss S. Lenglen and Miss E. Ryan
Mrs. Lambert Chambers and Mrs. D. R. Larcombe

1920 Miss S. Lenglen and Miss E. Ryan
Mrs. Lambert Chambers and Mrs. D. R. Larcombe

1921 Miss S. Lenglen and Miss E. Ryan
Mrs. A. E. Beamish and Mrs. G. E. Peacock

1922 Miss S. Lenglen and Miss E. Ryan
Mrs. A. D. Stocks and Miss K. McKane

1923 Miss S. Lenglen and Miss E. Ryan
Miss J. Austin and Miss E. L. Colyer

1924 Mrs. H. Wightman and Miss H. Wills
Mrs. B. C. Covell and Miss K. McKane

1925 Miss S. Lenglen and Miss E. Ryan
Mrs. A. V. Bridge and Mrs. C. G. McIlquham

1926 Miss E. Ryan and Miss M. K. Browne
Mrs. L. A. Godfree and Miss E. L. Colyer

1927 Miss H. Wills and Miss E. Ryan
Miss E. L. Heine and Mrs. G. E. Peacock

1928 Mrs. Holcroft-Watson and Miss P. Saunders
Miss E. H. Harvey and Miss E. Bennett

1929 Mrs. Holcroft-Watson and Mrs. L.R.C. Michell
Mrs. B. C. Covell and Mrs. D. C. Shepherd-Barron

1930 Mrs. F. S. Moody and Miss E. Ryan
Miss E. Cross and Miss S. Palfrey

1931 Mrs.D.C. Shepherd-Barron and Miss P.E. Mudford
Miss D. Metaxa and Miss J. Sigart

1932 Miss D. Metaxa and Miss J. Sigart
Miss E. Ryan and Miss H. H. Jacobs

1933 Mrs. R. Mathieu and Miss E. Ryan
Miss F. James and Miss A. M. Yorke

1934 Mrs. R. Mathieu and Miss E. Ryan
Mrs. D. Andrus and Mrs. S. Henrotin

1935 Miss F. James and Miss K. E. Stammers
Mrs. R. Mathieu and Mrs S. Sperling

1936 Miss F. James and Miss K. E. Stammers
Mrs. S. P. Fabyan and Miss H. H. Jacobs

1937 Mrs. R. Mathieu and Miss A. M. Yorke
Mrs. M. R. King and Mrs. J. B. Pittman

1938 Mrs. S. P. Fabyan and Miss A. Marble
Mrs. R. Mathieu and Miss A. M. Yorke

1939 Mrs S. P. Fabyan and Miss A. Marble
Miss H. H. Jacobs and Miss A. M. Yorke

1946 Miss L. Brough and Miss M. Osborne
Miss P. Betz and Miss D. Hart

1947 Miss D. Hart and Mrs. P. C. Todd
Miss L. Brough and Miss M. Osborne

1948 Miss L. Brough and Mrs. W. du Pont
Miss D. Hart and Mrs. P. C. Todd

1949 Miss L. Brough and Mrs. W. du Pont
Miss G. Moran and Mrs. P. C. Todd

1950 Miss L. Brough and Mrs. W. du Pont
Miss S. Fry and Miss D. Hart

1951 Miss S. Fry and Miss D. Hart
Miss L. Brough and Mrs. W. du Pont

1952 Miss S. Fry and Miss D. Hart
Miss L. Brough and Miss M. Connolly

1953 Miss S. Fry and Miss D. Hart
Miss M. Connolly and Miss J. Sampson

1954 Miss L. Brough and Mrs. W. du Pont
Miss S. Fry and Miss D. Hart

1955 Miss A. Mortimer and Miss J. A. Shilcock
Miss S. J. Bloomer and Miss P. E. Ward

1956 Miss A. Buxton and Miss A. Gibson
Miss F. Muller and Miss D. G. Seeney

1957 Miss A. Gibson and Miss D. R. Hard
Mrs. K. Hawton and Mrs. T. D. Long

1958 Miss M. E. Bueno and Miss A. Gibson
Mrs. W. du Pont and Miss M. Varner

1959 Miss J. Arth and Miss D. R. Hard
Mrs. J. G. Fleitz and Miss C. C. Truman

1960 Miss M. E. Bueno and Miss D. R. Hard
Miss S. Reynolds and Miss R. Schuurman

1961 Miss K. Hantze and Miss B. J. Moffitt
Miss J. Lehane and Miss M. Smith

1962 Miss B. J. Moffitt and Mrs. J. R. Susman
Mrs. L. E. G. Price and Miss R. Schuurman

1963 Miss M. E. Bueno and Miss D. R. Hard
Miss R. A. Ebbern and Miss M. Smith

1964 Miss M. Smith and Miss L. R. Turner
Miss B. J. Moffitt and Mrs. J. R. Susman

1965 Miss M. E. Bueno and Miss B. J. Moffitt
Miss F. Durr and Miss J. LieVrig

1966 Miss M. E. Bueno and Miss N. Richey
Miss M. Smith and Miss J. A. M. Tegart

1967 Miss R. Casals and Mrs. L. W. King
Miss M. E. Bueno and Miss N. Richey

1968 Miss R. Casals and Mrs. L. W. King
Miss F. Durr and Mrs. P. F. Jones

1969 Mrs. B. M. Court and Miss J. A. M. Tegart
Miss P. S. A. Hogan and Miss M. Michel

1970 Miss R. Casals and Mrs. L. W. King
Miss F. Durr and Miss S. V. Wade

1971 Miss R. Casals and Mrs. L. W. King
Mrs. B. M. Court and Miss E. F. Goolagong

1972 Mrs. L. W. King and Miss B. F. Stove
Mrs. D. E. Dalton and Miss F. Durr

1973 Miss R. Casals and Mrs. L. W. King
Miss F. Durr and Miss B. F. Stove

1974 Miss E. F. Goolagong and Miss M. Michel
Miss H. F. Gourlay and Miss K. M. Krantzcke

1975 Miss A. Kiyomura and Miss K. Sawamatsu
Miss F. Durr and Miss B. F. Stove

1976 Miss C. M. Evert and Miss M. Navratilova
Mrs. L. W. King and Miss B. F. Stove

1977 Mrs. H. F. Gourlay Cawley and Miss J. C. Russell
Miss M. Navratilova and Miss B. F . Stove

1978 Mrs. G. E. Reid and Miss. W. M. Turnbull
Miss M. Jausovec and Miss V. Ruzici

1979 Mrs. L. W. King and Miss M. Navratilova
Miss B. F. Stove and Miss W. M. Turnbull

1980 Miss K. Jordan and Miss A. E. Smith
Miss R. Casals and Miss W. M. Turnbull

1981 Miss M. Navratilova and Miss P. H. Shriver
Miss K. Jordan and Miss A. E. Smith

1982 Miss M. Navratilova and Miss P. H. Shriver
Miss K. Jordan and Miss A. E. Smith

1983 Miss M. Navratilova and Miss P. H. Shriver
Miss R. Casals and Miss W. M. Turnbull

1984 Miss M. Navratilova and Miss P. H. Shriver
Miss K. Jordan and Miss A. E. Smith

1985 Miss K. Jordan and Mrs. P. D. Smylie
Miss M. Navratilova and Miss P. H. Shriver

1986 Miss M. Navratilova and Miss P. H. Shriver
Miss H. Mandlikova and Miss W. M. Turnbull

1987 Miss C. Kohde-Kilsch and Miss H. Sukova
Miss B. Nagelsen and Mrs. P. D. Smylie

1988 Miss S. Graf and Miss G. Sabatini
Miss L. Savchenko and Miss N. Zvereva

1989 Miss J. Novotna and Miss H. Sukova
Miss L. Savchenko and Miss N. Zvereva

1990 Miss J. Novotna and Miss H. Sukova
Miss K. Jordan and Mrs. P. D. Smylie

1991 Miss L. Savchenko and Miss N. Zvereva
Miss G. Fernandez and Miss J. Novotna

1992 Miss G. Fernandez and Miss N. Zvereva
Miss J. Novotna and Mrs. L. Savchenko-Neiland

1993 Miss G. Fernandez and Miss N. Zvereva
Mrs. L. Neiland and Miss J. Novotna

1994 Miss G. Fernandez and Miss N. Zvereva
Miss J. Novotna and Miss A. Sanchez Vicario

1995 Miss J. Novotna and Miss A. Sanchez Vicario
Miss G. Fernandez and Miss N. Zvereva

1996 Miss M. Hingis and Miss H. Sukova
Miss M.J. McGrath and Mrs. L. Neiland

1997 Miss G. Fernandez and Miss N. Zvereva
Miss N.J. Arendt and Miss M.M. Bollegraf

1998 Miss M. Hingis and Miss J. Novotna
Miss L.A. Davenport and Miss N. Zvereva

1999 Miss L.A. Davenport and Miss C. Morariu
Miss M. de Swardt and Miss E. Tatarkova

2000 Miss S. Williams and Miss V. Williams
Mrs J. Halard–Decugis and Miss A. Sugiyama

2001 Miss L.M. Raymond and Miss R.P. Stubbs
Miss K. Clijsters and Miss A. Sugiyama

2002 Miss S. Williams and Miss V. Williams
Miss V. Ruano Pascual and Miss P. Suarez

2003 Miss K. Clijsters and Miss A. Sugiyama
Miss V. Ruano Pascual and Miss P. Suarez

2004 Miss C. Black and Miss R.P. Stubbs
Mrs L. Huber and Miss A. Sugiyama

2005 Miss C. Black and Mrs L. Huber
Miss S. Kuznetsova and Miss A. Muresmo

2006 Miss Z. Yan and Miss J. Zheng
Miss V. Ruano Pascual and Miss P. Suarez

2007 Miss C. Black and Mrs L. Huber
Miss K. Srebotnik and Miss A. Sugiyama

2008 Miss S. Williams and Miss V. Williams
Miss L.M. Raymond and Miss S. Stosur

2009 Miss S. Williams and Miss V. Williams
Miss S. Stosur and Miss R.P. Stubbs

2010 Miss V. King & Miss Y. Shvedova
Miss E. Vesnina & Miss V. Zvonareva

THE CHAMPIONSHIP ROLL
MIXED DOUBLES—CHAMPIONS & RUNNERS UP

1913	H. Crisp and Mrs. C. O. Tuckey *J. C. Parke and Mrs. D. R. Larcombe*	1953	V. Seixas and Miss D. Hart *E. Morea and Miss S. Fry*	1983	J. M. Lloyd and Miss W. M. Turnbull *S. Denton and Mrs. L. W. King*
1914	J. C. Parke and Mrs. D.R. Larcombe *A. F. Wilding and Miss M. Broquedis*	1954	V. Seixas and Miss D. Hart *K. R. Rosewall and Mrs. W. du Pont*	1984	J. M. Lloyd and Miss W. M. Turnbull *S. Denton and Miss K. Jordan*
1919	R. Lycett and Miss E. Ryan *A. D. Prebble and Mrs. Lambert Chambers*	1955	V. Seixas and Miss D. Hart *E. Morea and Miss L. Brough*	1985	P. McNamee and Miss M. Navratilova *J. B. Fitzgerald and Mrs. P. D. Smylie*
1920	G. L. Patterson and Miss S. Lenglen *R. Lycett and Miss E. Ryan*	1956	V. Seixas and Miss S. Fry *G. Mulloy and Miss A. Gibson*	1986	K. Flach and Miss K. Jordan *H. P. Guenthardt and Miss M. Navratilova*
1921	R. Lycett and Miss E. Ryan *M. Woosnam and Miss P. L. Howkins*	1957	M. G. Rose and Miss D. R. Hard *N. A. Fraser and Miss A. Gibson*	1987	M. J. Bates and Miss J. M. Durie *D. Cahill and Miss N. Provis*
1922	P. O'Hara-Wood and Miss S. Lenglen *R. Lycett and Miss E. Ryan*	1958	R. N. Howe and Miss L. Coghlan *K. Nielsen and Miss A. Gibson*	1988	S. E. Stewart and Miss Z. L. Garrison *K. Jones and Mrs. S. W. Magers*
1923	R. Lycett and Miss E. Ryan *L. S. Deane and Mrs. D. C. Shepherd-Barron*	1959	R. Laver and Miss D. R. Hard *N. A. Fraser and Miss M. E. Bueno*	1989	J. Pugh and Miss J. Novotna *M. Kratzmann and Miss J. M. Byrne*
1924	J. B. Gilbert and Miss K. McKane *L. A. Godfree and Mrs. D. C. Shepherd-Barron*	1960	R. Laver and Miss D. R. Hard *R. N. Howe and Miss M. E. Bueno*	1990	R. Leach and Miss Z. L. Garrison *J. B. Fitzgerald and Mrs P. D. Smylie*
1925	J. Borotra and Miss S. Lenglen *H. L. de Morpurgo and Miss E. Ryan*	1961	F. S. Stolle and Miss L. R. Turner *R. N. Howe and Miss E. Buding*	1991	J. B. Fitzgerald and Mrs. P. D. Smylie *J. Pugh and Miss N. Zvereva*
1926	L. A. Godfree and Mrs. L. A. Godfree *H. Kinsey and Miss M. K. Browne*	1962	N. A. Fraser and Mrs. W. du Pont *R. D. Ralston and Miss A. S. Haydon*	1992	C. Suk and Mrs L. Savchenko-Neiland *J. Eltingh and Miss M. Oremans*
1927	F. T. Hunter and Miss E. Ryan *L. A. Godfree and Mrs. L. A. Godfree*	1963	K. N. Fletcher and Miss M. Smith *R. A. J. Hewitt and Miss D. R. Hard*	1993	M. Woodforde and Miss M. Navratilova *T. Nijssen and Miss M. M. Bollegraf*
1928	P. D. B. Spence and Miss E. Ryan *J. Crawford and Miss D. Akhurst*	1964	F. S. Stolle and Miss L. R. Turner *K. N. Fletcher and Miss M. Smith*	1994	T. A. Woodbridge and Miss H. Sukova *T. J. Middleton and Miss L. M. McNeil*
1929	F. T. Hunter and Miss H. Wills *I. G. Collins and Miss J. Fry*	1965	K. N. Fletcher and Miss M. Smith *A. D. Roche and Miss J. A. M. Tegart*	1995	J. Stark and Miss M. Navratilova *C. Suk and Miss G. Fernandez*
1930	J. H. Crawford and Miss E. Ryan *D. Prenn and Miss H. Krahwinkel*	1966	K. N. Fletcher and Miss M. Smith *R. D. Ralston amd Mrs. L. W. King*	1996	C. Suk and Miss H. Sukova *M. Woodforde and Mrs. L. Neiland*
1931	G. M. Lott and Mrs L. A. Harper *I. G. Collins and Miss J. C. Ridley*	1967	O. K. Davidson and Mrs. L. W. King *K. N. Fletcher and Miss M. E. Bueno*	1997	C. Suk and Miss H. Sukova *A. Olhovskiy and Mrs L. Neiland*
1932	E. Maier and Miss E. Ryan *H. C. Hopman and Miss J. Sigart*	1968	K. N. Fletcher and Mrs. B. M. Court *A. Metreveli and Miss O. Morozova*	1998	M. Mirnyi and Miss S. Williams *M. Bhupathi and Miss M. Lucic*
1933	G. von Cramm and Miss H. Krahwinkel *N. G. Farquharson and Miss M. Heeley*	1969	F. S. Stolle and Mrs. P. F. Jones *A. D. Roche and Miss J. A. M. Tegart*	1999	L. Paes and Miss L.M. Raymond *J. Bjorkman and Miss A. Kournikova*
1934	R. Miki and Miss D. E. Round *H. W. Austin and Mrs D. C. Shepherd-Barron*	1970	I. Nastase and Miss R. Casals *A. Metreveli and Miss O. Morozova*	2000	D. Johnson and Miss K. Po *L. Hewitt and Miss K. Clijsters*
1935	F. J. Perry and Miss D. E. Round *H. C. Hopman and Mrs. H. C. Hopman*	1971	O. K. Davidson and Mrs. L. W. King *M. C. Riessen and Mrs. B. M. Court*	2001	L. Friedl and Miss D. Hantuchova *M. Bryan and Mrs L. Huber*
1936	F. J. Perry and Miss D. E. Round *J. D. Budge and Mrs. S. P. Fabyan*	1972	I. Nastase and Miss R. Casals *K.G. Warwick and Miss E. F. Goolagong*	2002	M. Bhupathi and Miss E. Likhovtseva *K. Ullyett and Miss D. Hantuchova*
1937	J. D. Budge and Miss A. Marble *Y. Petra and Mrs. R. Mathieu*	1973	O. K. Davidson and Mrs. L. W. King *R. Ramirez and Miss J. S. Newberry*	2003	L. Paes and Miss M. Navratilova *A. Ram and Miss A. Rodionova*
1938	J. D. Budge and Miss A. Marble *H. Henkel and Mrs. S. P. Fabyan*	1974	O. K. Davidson and Mrs. L. W. King *M. J. Farrell and Miss L. J. Charles*	2004	W. Black and Miss C. Black *T.A. Woodbridge and Miss A. Molik*
1939	R. L. Riggs and Miss A. Marble *F. H. D. Wilde and Miss N. B. Brown*	1975	M. C. Riessen and Mrs. B. M. Court *A. J. Stone and Miss B. F. Stove*	2005	M. Bhupathi and Miss M. Pierce *P. Hanley and Miss T. Perebiynis*
1946	T. Brown and Miss L. Brough *G. E. Brown and Miss D. Bundy*	1976	A. D. Roche and Miss F. Durr *R. L. Stockton and Miss R. Casals*	2006	A. Ram and Miss V. Zvonareva *B. Bryan and Miss V. Williams*
1947	J. E. Bromwich and Miss L. Brough *C. F. Long and Mrs. N. M. Bolton*	1977	R. A. J. Hewitt and Miss G. R. Stevens *F. D. McMillan and Miss B. F. Stove*	2007	J. Murray and Miss J. Jankovic *J. Bjorkman and Miss A. Molik*
1948	J. E. Bromwich and Miss L. Brough *F. A. Sedgman and Miss D. Hart*	1978	F. D. McMillan and Miss B. F. Stove *R. O. Ruffels and Mrs. L. W. King*	2008	B. Bryan and Miss S. Stosur *M. Bryan and Miss K. Srebotnik*
1949	E. W. Sturgess and Mrs. S. P. Summers *J. E. Bromwich and Miss L. Brough*	1979	R. A. J. Hewitt and Miss G. R. Stevens *F. D. McMillan and Miss B. F. Stove*	2009	M. Knowles and Miss A-L. Groenefeld *L. Paes and Miss C. Black*
1950	E. W. Sturgess and Miss L. Brough *G. E. Brown and Mrs. P. C. Todd*	1980	J. R. Austin and Miss T. Austin *M. R. Edmondson and Miss D. L. Fromholtz*	2010	L. Paes & Miss C. Black *W. Moody & Miss L. Raymond*
1951	F. A. Sedgman and Miss D. Hart *M. G. Rose and Mrs. N. M. Bolton*	1981	F. D. McMillan and Miss B. F. Stove *J. R. Austin and Miss T. Austin*		
1952	F. A. Sedgman and Miss D. Hart *E. Morea and Mrs. T. D. Long*	1982	K. Curren and Miss A. E. Smith *J. M. Lloyd and Miss W. M. Turnbull*		

THE CHAMPIONSHIP ROLL

BOYS' SINGLES

1947 K. Nielsen (DENMARK)
S. V. Davidson (SWEDEN)

1948 S. Stockenberg (SWEDEN)
D. Vad (HUNGARY)

1949 S. Stockenberg (SWEDEN)
J. A.T. Horn (GBR)

1950 J. A.T. Horn (GBR)
K. Mobarek (EGYPT)

1951 J. Kupferburger (SA)
K. Mobarek (EGYPT)

1952 R. K. Wilson (GBR)
T. T. Fancutt (SA)

1953 W. A. Knight (GBR)
R. Krishnan (INDIA)

1954 R. Krishnan (INDIA)
A. J. Cooper (AUSTRALIA)

1955 M. P. Hann (GBR)
J. E. Lundquist (SWEDEN)

1956 R. Holmberg (USA)
R. G. Laver (AUSTRALIA)

1957 J. I. Tattersall (GBR)
I. Ribeiro (BRAZIL)

1958 E. Buchholz (USA)
P. J. Lall (INDIA)

1959 T. Lejus (USSR)
R. W. Barnes (BRAZIL)

1960 A. R. Mandelstam (SA)
J. Mukerjea (INDIA)

1961 C. E. Graebner (USA)
E. Blanke (AUSTRIA)

1962 S. Matthews (GBR)
A. Metreveli (USSR)

1963 N. Kalogeropoulos (GREECE)
I. El Shafei (UAR)

1964 I. El Shafei (UAR)
V. Korotkov (USSR)

1965 V. Korotkov (USSR)
G. Goven (FRANCE)

1966 V. Korotkov (USSR)
B. E. Fairlie (NZ)

1967 M. Orantes (SPAIN)
M. S. Estep (USA)

1968 J. G. Alexander (AUSTRALIA)
J. Thamin (FRANCE)

1969 B. Bertram (SA)
J. G. Alexander (AUSTRALIA)

1970 B. Bertram (SA)
F. Gebert (GERMANY)

1971 R. Kreiss (USA)
S. A. Warboys (GBR)

1972 B. Borg (SWEDEN)
C. J. Mottram (GBR)

1973 W. Martin (USA)
C. S. Dowdeswell (RHODESIA)

1974 W. Martin (USA)
Ash Amritraj (INDIA)

1975 C. J. Lewis (NZ)
R. Ycaza (ECUADOR)

1976 H. Guenthardt (SWITZERLAND)
P. Elter (GERMANY)

1977 V. A. Winitsky (USA)
T. E. Teltscher (USA)

1978 I. Lendl (CZECHOSLOVAKIA)
J. Turpin (USA)

1979 R. Krishnan (INDIA)
D. Siegler (USA)

1980 T. Tulasne (FRANCE)
H. D. Beutel (GERMANY)

1981 M. W. Anger (USA)
P. Cash (AUSTRALIA)

1982 P. Cash (AUSTRALIA)
H. Sundstrom (SWEDEN)

1983 S. Edberg (SWEDEN)
J. Frawley (AUSTRALIA)

1984 M.Kratzmann (AUSTRALIA)
S. Kruger (SA)

1985 L. Lavalle (MEXICO)
E. Velez (MEXICO)

1986 E. Velez (MEXICO)
J. Sanchez (SPAIN)

1987 D. Nargiso (ITALY)
J. R. Stoltenberg (AUSTRALIA)

1988 N. Pereira (VENEZUELA)
G. Raoux (FRANCE)

1989 N. Kulti (SWEDEN)
T. A. Woodbridge (AUSTRALIA)

1990 L. Paes (INDIA)
M. Ondruska (SA)

1991 T. Enquist (SWEDEN)
M. Joyce (USA)

1992 D. Skoch (CZECHOSLOVAKIA)
B. Dunn (USA)

1993 R. Sabau (ROMANIA)
J. Szymanski (VENEZUELA)

1994 S. Humphries (USA)
M. A. Philippoussis (AUSTRALIA)

1995 O. Mutis (FRANCE)
N. Kiefer (GERMANY)

1996 V. Voltchkov (BELARUS)
I. Ljubicic (CROATIA)

1997 W. Whitehouse (SOUTH AFRICA)
D. Elsner (GERMANY)

1998 R. Federer (SWITZERLAND)
I. Labadze (GEORGIA)

1999 J. Melzer (AUSTRIA)
K. Pless (DENMARK)

2000 N. Mahut (FRANCE)
M. Ancic (CROATIA)

2001 R. Valent (SWITZERLAND)
G. Muller (LUXEMBOURG)

2002 T. Reid (AUSTRALIA)
L. Quahab (ALGERIA)

2003 F. Mergea (ROMANIA)
C. Guccione (AUSTRALIA)

2004 G. Monfils (FRANCE)
M. Kasiri (GBR)

2005 J. Chardy (FRANCE)
R. Haase (NETHERLANDS)

2006 T. De Bakker (NETHERLANDS)
M. Gawron (POLAND)

2007 D. Young (USA)
V. Ignatic (BELARUS)

2008 G. Dimitrov (BULGARIA)
H. Kontinen (FINLAND)

2009 A. Kuznetsov (RUSSIA)
J. Cox (USA)

2010 M. Fucsovics (HUNGARY)
B. Mitchell (AUSTRALIA)

BOYS' DOUBLES

1982 P. Cash and J. Frawley
R. D. Leach and J. J. Ross

1983 M. Kratzmann and S. Youl
M. Nastase and O. Rahnasto

1984 R. Brown and R. Weiss
M. Kratzmann and J. Svensson

1985 A. Moreno and J. Yzaga
P. Korda and C. Suk

1986 T. Carbonell and P. Korda
S. Barr and H. Karrasch

1987 J. Stoltenberg and T. Woodbridge
D. Nargiso and E. Rossi

1988 J. Stoltenberg and T. Woodbridge
D. Rikl and T. Zdrazila

1989 J. Palmer and J. Stark
J-L. De Jager and W. R. Ferreira

1990 S. Lareau and S. Leblanc
C. Marsh and M. Ondruska

1991 K. Alami and G. Rusedski
J-L. De Jager and A. Medvedev

1992 S. Baldas and S. Draper
M. S. Bhupathi and N. Kirtane

1993 S. Downs and J. Greenhalgh
N. Godwin and G. Williams

1994 B. Ellwood and M. Philippoussis
V. Platenik and R. Schlachter

1995 M. Lee and J.M. Trotman
A. Hernandez and M. Puerta

1996 D. Bracciali and J. Robichaud
D. Roberts and W. Whitehouse

1997 L. Horna and N. Massu
J. Van de Westhuizen and W. Whitehouse

1998 R. Federer and O. Rochus
M. Llodra and A. Ram

1999 G. Coria and D. Nalbandian
T. Enev and J. Nieminem

2000 D. Coene and K. Vliegen
A. Banks and B. Riby

2001 F. Dancevic and G. Lapentti
B. Echagaray and S. Gonzales

2002 F. Mergea and H. Tecau
B. Baker and B. Ram

2003 F. Mergea and H. Tecau
A. Feeney and C. Guccione

2004 B. Evans and S. Oudsema
R. Haase and V. Troicki

2005 J. Levine and M. Shabaz
S. Groth and A. Kennaugh

2006 K. Damico and N. Schnugg
M. Klizan and A. Martin

2007 D. Lopez and M. Trevisan
R. Jebavy and M. Klizan

2008 C-P. Hsieh and T-H. Yang
M. Reid and B. Tomic

2009 P-H. Herbert and K. Krawietz
J. Obry and A. Puget

2010 L. Broady & T. Farquharson
L. Burton & G. Morgan

GIRLS' SINGLES

1947 Miss G. Domken (BELGIUM)
Miss B. Wallen (SWEDEN)

1948 Miss O. Miskova (CZECHOSLOVAKIA)
Miss V. Rigollet (SWITZERLAND)

1949 Miss C. Mercelis (BELGIUM)
Miss J. S. V. Partridge (GBR)

1950 Miss L. Cornell (GBR)
Miss A. Winter (NORWAY)

1951 Miss L. Cornell (GBR)
Miss S. Lazzarino (ITALY)

1952 Miss F. J. I. ten Bosch (NETHERLANDS)
Miss R. Davar (INDIA)

1953 Miss D. Kilian (SA)
Miss V. A. Pitt (GBR)

1954 Miss V. A. Pitt (GBR)
Miss C. Monnot (FRANCE)

1955 Miss S. M. Armstrong (GBR)
Miss B. de Chambure (FRANCE)

1956 Miss A. S. Haydon (GBR)
Miss I. Buding (GERMANY)

1957 Miss M. Arnold (USA)
Miss E. Reyes (MEXICO)

1958 Miss S. M. Moore (USA)
Miss A. Dmitrieva (USSR)

1959 Miss J. Cross (SA)
Miss D. Schuster (AUSTRIA)

1960 Miss K. Hantze (USA)
Miss L. M Hutchings (SA)

1961 Miss G. Baksheeva (USSR)
Miss K. D. Chabot (USA)

1962 Miss G. Baksheeva (USSR)
Miss E. P. Terry (NZ)

1963 Miss D. M. Salfati (FRANCE)
Miss K. Dening (AUSTRALIA)

1964 Miss P. Bartkowicz (USA)
Miss E. Subirats (MEXICO)

1965 Miss O. Morozova (USSR)
Miss R. Giscarfe (ARGENTINA)

1966 Miss B. Lindstrom (FINLAND)
Miss J. A. Congdon (GBR)

1967 Miss J. Salome (NETHERLANDS)
Miss E. M. Strandberg (SWEDEN)

1968 Miss K. Pigeon (USA)
Miss L. E. Hunt (AUSTRALIA)

1969 Miss K. Sawamatsu (JAPAN)
Miss B. I. Kirk (SA)

1970 Miss S. Walsh (USA)
Miss M. V. Kroshina (USSR)

1971 Miss M.V. Kroshina (USSR)
Miss S. H. Minford (GBR)

1972 Miss I. Kloss (SA)
Miss G. L. Coles (GBR)

1973 Miss A. Kiyomura (USA)
Miss M. Navratilova (CZECHOSLOVAKIA)

1974 Miss M. Jausovec (YUGOSLAVIA)
Miss M. Simionescu (ROMANIA)

1975 Miss N. Y. Chmyreva (USSR)
Miss R. Marsikova (CZECHOSLOVAKIA)

1976 Miss N. Y. Chmyreva (USSR)
Miss M. Kruger (SA)

1977 Miss L. Antonoplis (USA)
Miss Mareen Louie (USA)

1978 Miss T. Austin (USA)
Miss H. Mandlikova (CZECHOSLOVAKIA)

1979 Miss M. L. Piatek (USA)
Miss A. A. Moulton (USA)

1980 Miss D. Freeman (AUSTRALIA)
Miss S. J. Leo (AUSTRALIA)

1981 Miss Z. Garrison (USA)
Miss R. R. Uys (SA)

1982 Miss C. Tanvier (FRANCE)
Miss H. Sukova (CZECHOSLOVAKIA)

1983 Miss P. Paradis (FRANCE)
Miss P. Hy (HONG KONG)

1984 Miss A. N. Croft (GBR)
Miss E. Reinach (SA)

1985 Miss A. Holikova (CZECHOSLOVAKIA)
Miss J. M. Byrne (AUSTRALIA)

1986 Miss N.M. Zvereva (USSR)
Miss L. Meskhi (USSR)

1987 Miss N.M. Zvereva (USSR)
Miss J. Halard (FRANCE)

1988 Miss B. Schultz (NETHERLANDS)
Miss E. Derly (FRANCE)

1989 Miss A. Strnadova (CZECHOSLAVAKIA)
Miss M. J. McGrath (USA)

1990 Miss A. Strnadova (CZECHOSLAVAKIA)
Miss K. Sharpe (AUSTRALIA)

1991 Miss B. Rittner (GERMANY)
Miss E. Makarova (USSR)

1992 Miss C. Rubin (USA)
Miss L. Courtois (BELGIUM)

1993 Miss N. Feber (BELGIUM)
Miss R. Grande (ITALY)

1994 Miss M. Hingis (SWITZERLAND)
Miss M-R. Jeon (KOREA)

1995 Miss A. Olsza (POLAND)
Miss T. Tanasugarn (THAILAND)

1996 Miss A. Mauresmo (FRANCE)
Miss M. L. Serna (SPAIN)

1997 Miss C. Black (ZIMBABWE)
Miss A. Rippner (USA)

1998 Miss K. Srebotnik (SLOVENIA)
Miss K. Clijsters (BELGIUM)

1999 Miss I. Tulyagnova (UZBEKHISTAN)
Miss L. Krasnoroutskaya (USSR)

2000 Miss M. E. Salerni (ARGENTINA)
Miss T. Perebiynis (UKRAINE)

2001 Miss A. Widjaja (INDONESIA)
Miss D. Safina (USSR)

2002 Miss V. Douchevina (RUSSIA)
Miss M. Sharapova (USSR)

2003 Miss K. Flipkens (BELGIUM)
Miss A. Tchakvetadze (USSR)

2004 Miss K. Bondarenko (UKRAINE)
Miss A. Ivanovic (SERBIA AND MONTENEGRO)

2005 Miss A. Radwanska (POLAND)
Miss T. Paszek (AUSTRIA)

2006 Miss C. Wozniacki (DENMARK)
Miss M. Rybarikova (SLOVAKIA)

2007 Miss U. Radwanska (POLAND)
Miss M. Brengle (USA)

2008 Miss L. Robson (GBR)
Miss N. Lertcheewakarn (THAILAND)

2009 Miss N. Lertcheewakarn (THAILAND)
Miss K. Mladenovic (FRANCE)

2010 Miss K. Pliskova (CZECH REPUBLIC)
Miss S. Ishizu (JAPAN)

GIRLS' DOUBLES

1982 Miss B. Herr and Miss P. Barg
Miss B. S. Gerken and Miss G. A. Rush

1983 Miss P. Fendick and Miss P. Hy
Miss C. Anderholm and Miss H. Olsson

1984 Miss C. Kuhlman and Miss S. Rehe
Miss V. Milvidskaya and Miss L. I. Savchenko

1985 Miss L. Field and Miss J. Thompson
Miss E. Reinach and Miss J. A. Richardson

1986 Miss M. Jaggard and Miss L. O'Neill
Miss L. Meskhi and Miss N. M. Zvereva

1987 Miss N. Medvedeva and Miss N.M. Zvereva
Miss I. S. Kim and Miss P. M. Moreno

1988 Miss J. A. Faull and Miss R. McQuillan
Miss A. Dechaume and Miss E. Derly

1989 Miss J. Capriati and Miss M. McGrath
Miss A. Strnadova and Miss E. Sviglerova

1990 Miss K. Habsudova and Miss A. Strnadova
Miss N. J. Pratt and Miss K. Sharpe

1991 Miss C. Barclay and Miss L. Zaltz
Miss J. Limmer and Miss A. Woolcock

1992 Miss M. Avotins and Miss L. McShea
Miss P. Nelson and Miss J. Steven

1993 Miss L. Courtois and Miss N. Feber
Miss H. Mochizuki and Miss Y. Yoshida

1994 Miss E. De Villiers and Miss E. E. Jelfs
Miss C. M. Morariu and Miss L. Varmuzova

1995 Miss C. Black and Miss A. Olsza
Miss T. Musgrove and Miss J Richardson

1996 Miss O. Barabanschikova and Miss A. Mauresmo
Miss L. Osterloh and Miss S. Reeves

1997 Miss C. Black and Miss I. Selyutina
Miss M. Matevzic and Miss K. Srebotnik

1998 Miss E. Dyrberg and Miss J. Kostanic
Miss P. Rampre and Miss I. Tulyaganova

1999 Miss D. Bedanova and Miss M.E. Salerni
Miss T. Perebiynis and Miss I. Tulyaganova

2000 Miss I. Gaspar and Miss T. Perebiynis
Miss D. Bedanova and Miss M. E. Salerni

2001 Miss G. Dulko and Miss A. Harkleroad
Miss C. Horiatopoulos and Miss B. Mattek

2002 Miss E. Clijsters and Miss B. Strycova
Miss A. Baker and Miss A-L. Groenfeld

2003 Miss A. Kleybanova and Miss S. Mirza
Miss K. Bohmova and Miss M. Krajicek

2004 Miss V. Azarenka and Miss V. Havartsova
Miss M. Erakovic and Miss M. Niculescu

2005 Miss V. Azarenka and Miss A. Szavay
Miss M. Erakovic and Miss M. Niculescu

2006 Miss A. Kleybanova and Miss A. Pavlyuchenkova
Miss K. Antoniychuk and Miss A. Dulgheru

2007 Miss A. Pavlyuchenkova and Miss U. Radwanska
Miss M. Doi and Miss K. Nara

2008 Miss P. Hercog and Miss J. Moore
Miss I. Holland and Miss S. Peers

2009 Miss N. Lertcheewakarn and Miss S. Peers
Miss K. Mladenovic and Miss S. Njiric

2010 Miss T. Babos and Miss S. Stephens
Miss I. Khromacheva and Miss E. Svitolina